If You Listen Really Hard, God Will Tell You Stories

If You Listen Really Hard, God Will Tell You Stories

by
Jane Wolford Hughes

Foreword by David Gibson
Introduction by John Shea

Saint Mary's Press
Christian Brothers Publications
Winona, Minnesota

The publishing team for this book included Carl Koch, FSC, development editor; Barbara Augustyn Sirovatka, copy editor and typesetter; Barbara Bartelson, production editor; Stephan Nagel, art director; Diana Witt, indexer, Tim Foley, illustrator; pre-press, printing, and binding by the graphics division of Saint Mary's Press.

The acknowledgments continue on page 144.

Printed in the United States of America

Printing: 9 8 7 6 5 47 3 2 1

Year: 2003 02 01 00 99 98 97 96 95

ISBN 0-88489-352-9

 Genuine recycled paper with 10% post-consumer waste. Printed with soy-based ink.

Contents

Foreword

What is remarkable about Jane Wolford Hughes' stories of faith is their power to reveal to readers the sheer possibility of living as a Christian in the world—to illustrate what faith "looks like," even in complex contemporary circumstances.

An added benefit of Jane Hughes' storytelling derives from her willingness to "identify" with her readers as real people. It is as if she were saying to readers: "I've experienced predicaments and struggles, disappointments and successes, similar to those you experience. Here's what happened and how I view these events in the light of faith."

The result, I hope, is that many readers will see reflections of themselves and their life experiences in her stories.

I know Jane Hughes best as a longtime contributor of stories to Faith Alive!—the religious education series Catholic News Service (CNS) creates for diocesan newspapers. Most stories in this book originally were developed for Faith Alive!

To say that I value Jane Hughes' contributions greatly would be an understatement. She writes compellingly, drawing not only upon her adult religious education expertise but upon vivid memories of people she has known at every stage of her life.

At CNS we regard such stories of faith as essential to Faith Alive! True stories are interesting, after all. They capture readers' attention. Furthermore, the storyteller can uniquely show that Christianity is not just a fine set of ideas. Faith is a way to live.

As Jane Hughes writes: "I asked a veteran religious educator how to teach Christian love. Her answer was, 'You can't teach it, you have to "be" it.'"

These stories are about how to "be" a Christian in the context of life's ordinary events.

DAVID GIBSON
Editor, Faith Alive!
Catholic News Service

Preface

If readers can identify with persons in this collection of stories and gain strength and hope as they witness the power of prayer and the grace of God working, my efforts will be rewarded.

These stories were written on assignment on a specific theme or topic with space limitations and fixed deadlines as commissioned by the Catholic News Service for its Faith Alive! series. I am grateful to them for allowing the stories to be published in book form. The stories are not intentionally autobiographical, but they do reflect bits and snatches of my thinking, beliefs, and experiences. In some instances, names have been changed, but the facts are as true as I know them. Persons are featured because their unique responses to life illustrate the assigned topic.

More stories wander around in my head, waiting to gain a place on the printed page. They will emerge in due time. Since childhood, writing has been second nature to me. A great deal of what I have written does not bear my name. At fourteen, I wrote informational pamphlets for a missionary order; in high school, a weekly column on school news in the parish paper; and in college, a series of spiritual meditations. The editors of the latter felt that if readers thought the reflections had been written by a priest or sister, they would find them more authentic. The age of the laity had not arrived! Even after Vatican Council II, diocesan policy gave credit to the office rather than to the individual for the study and training materials that I had written, cowritten, or edited.

My writing has its roots in my life and the choices I have made: to be married, a mother, a stepmother, a housewife, a volunteer, an educator, a leader, and an activist. My arena has centered in the church. This is hardly surprising, having grown up as I did in a family where service in and through the church was normal and expected. Generations before me had set the direction, including a brave French Canadian grandmother who was part of the Underground Railroad that smuggled slaves across the Detroit River to Canada.

After two years of writing fashion copy for Detroit's largest department store, I felt that God was calling me to use my talents in other ways—to try to mend what is broken in society, to give a voice to the silent, to confront the powerful, to show compassion to those who live lives that are less than human. To say the decision was easy is to deny a young woman's romance with fashion, a subject that still continues to seduce. However, once the decision was made, the tug of my heritage held me anchored in the church, answering God's call by ministering in the world. I haven't regretted it. The church was and is my home. As in any human home, at times there is discord and a great need for dialog across the male-maintained-medieval-moat. I get angry; I grumble; but I won't run away.

In the past few years I have become interested in Benedictine spirituality. I especially relish Benedict's instruction in the Rule, "Listen with the ear of your heart." It is a lesson for everyone. As a writer, my spirit leans forward to hear what isn't said behind that which is, to seek the meaning in silences, to hear the truth in everyday miracles, to answer with tenderness the sob never uttered. Listening this way makes living a more abundant adventure, but it also reminds me that I will never live long enough to write of all the beauty shown to me by persons and nature. While so many people and experiences in nature may never end up in my stories, I treasure them all as glimpses into the everlasting love of God for us.

In the process of writing, I must draw apart in what the Quakers call "centering down." The insights they gain, they call "openings." From my "openings," stories are spun. My centering down is not always at the most convenient time or place. Meals can be delayed, and so can I. No one has mentioned that I should plan a little more realistically, so to my wonderfully understanding husband, Jack, and our children and grandchildren, I dedicate this book—just as I have dedicated my life.

JANE WOLFORD HUGHES

Introduction

On Roosters, Friends, and the Spirit

Above the door jamb on the inside of my office hangs a pair of brightly colored roosters held together by string. They used to hang in the Bombay Bicycle Club on Sanibel Island—I think. I received them in the mail many years ago. The accompanying note read, "My husband, Jack, and I had dinner in the Bombay Bicycle Club. Remember the East Coast Religious Education Conference?"

It all came back in a flash. It was a wonderful evening of food, drink, and conversation in the Bombay Bicycle Club in Washington, D.C. We did not solve all the problems of the world. But we were attentive enough to each other's words and respectful enough of each other's experience that the Spirit joined us and did what the Spirit always does—create friends.

The roosters were sent by Jane Wolford Hughes.

People come into my office, move the books off the chair, and sit down. We talk, do business, plot—whatever is called for. Then they turn around and see the roosters. "Where did you get those?"

I tell them the story. It differs a little bit every time I tell it—not because I am adding things, but because more things come to mind.

Often they say, "I've had conversations like that." And they proceed to share their story about friends in conversation and the release of the Spirit.

The Spirit is contagious. One story elicits another, and soon a Pentecost wind is stirring. But the experiences of the Spirit are also easily forgettable. They are left behind in the rush of time and in competition with new experiences. We need things like the roosters to remind us.

In this book Jane Wolford Hughes has created a wonderful series of "roosters." They are cameos, vignettes, snapshots, clips about people she has known, her friends in the Spirit. From each of them, both in their courage and their fragility, she has received a quickening of the Spirit and a measure of wisdom. In sharing them with us, our spirits are also quickened and our wisdom enhanced.

Someone once defined faith as holding in memory an experience that gives a warrant for hope. That is what these memories are—warrants for hope. They are not nostalgic or sentimental. They do not make us yearn for the past or set us adrift in reverie. They are a gathering of people yielding a gathering of insights that build the quiet strength we need to lean into the unknown future.

When the last page of this book is turned, we realize in a new way the ancient Christian truth: The flower of hope grows in the soil of struggle and in the company of friends.

JOHN SHEA

If You Listen Really Hard, God Will Tell You Stories

"God has many more stories to tell you."

In the waiting hour of twilight my grandfather taught me about silence. We fished in a small rowboat in an inland lake in Michigan until after the moon rose, glistening on the water. He had explained the rules of fishing to me, "Bait your own hook, sit still, and don't talk." The latter, "Because you will disturb the fish."

Each trip, the rules remained the same. We left behind the clutter of life in the cottage and, as we detached ourselves farther and farther from the shore, a new kind of peace came to us. Once his voice entered the silence, "If you listen really hard, God will tell you stories."

I listened. He was right. My mind envisioned new and exciting "somedays," and I came close to tears over the beauty of the starry night and the wondrous love of my family, both of which I knew but did not fully appreciate.

Gram'pa Gerbig had been a traveling salesman whose integrity, eloquence, and charm had brought him a good income. On the road he had been comforted by the companion he came to know so well—silence. He learned its secrets and was passing them on to me. Even though I was barely on the brink of adolescence, I felt privileged to have his friendship, which did not need words to sustain it.

After college graduation, I wrote fashion copy for Hudson's Department Store. Each morning Gram'pa drove me downtown on his way to work. After establishing the health of the members of each of our households, we settled comfortably into our caring, silent intimacy. It was a good way to start the day, letting "God tell us stories." The world we were about to enter would be noisy, and its demands would dig deeply into us. When we arrived at the employees' entrance he would kiss me good-bye and say, "You look lovely. You make me proud." And then, "God bless you!" I would say, "You too, Gram'pa!" and off he would go.

Some days my father would ride downtown with us, for Gram'pa now worked for him. Daddy caught the spirit of the refreshing quiet. The half hour passed with a sweetness that could only be described in that way. A few years later, Daddy and I would talk nostalgically about those rides and the gift of growing closer through the silence. In the long years after my mother died, my father and I were able to sit companionably quiet. He lived alone in a big house, insisting on continuing the pattern of his independence.

When my husband and I returned from the military service with Gram'pa's first great-grandchild, he acted as if he held a vision of immortality in his arms. He was enormously pleased, but characteristically thoughtful.

We lived in a very small house that Gram'pa named the "Doll House." He visited often, puttering around fixing things or weeding the garden as I did my chores. He had a fetish about knives. Mine were dull, which to him was one step removed from a cook's mortal sin. Whistling, he sharpened the knives on his stone at least once a month. Each visit, he would spend time holding Diane, humming little tunes and snatches of hymns.

One of his interests was his garden of strange, even exotic plants. He grew, grated, and produced his own horseradish. When he gave me my annual supply he warned, "This is hotter than Hades, so be careful!"

When Diane was walking he would take her for strolls to the park nearby, fit her into the little chair-swings, and push her gently. Occasionally he talked to her about the birds and flowers. I was surprised by his knowledge. I don't know whether their silences left a mark on Diane or if it is in her genes, for she grew up seeking, guarding, and relishing places of silence away from the bustle of her brothers and sisters.

In 1947 when I looked at Gram'pa in the casket with his red tie and his elegant suit, I grinned, remembering his old tan fishing sweater frayed at the sleeves. I sat next to the coffin, for I was carrying his second great-grandchild and standing was hard. I pondered all that he had taught me and was deep inside the quiet of myself when I heard him say gently, "God has many more stories to tell you." He was right again.

Mending All Kinds of Brokenness

*The sacrament of extreme unction only added to
my first innocent impression that the hour of death was the time
for this last-ditch effort to clean up your act.*

The grown-ups were suspended in a hush of silence like actors who had forgotten their lines. They were very solemn, hiding behind their faces that day so long ago when my Grandfather Ouellette was being anointed. He died soon after the priest left, and the grown-ups said it was good they hadn't waited any longer to call Father.

I was five then, but I could remember the discussions that had taken place about the "last rites" and not wanting to frighten Papa. I got the idea that whatever the priest did in that bedroom opened the window to death. My mother explained that the priest prepared Papa to meet God. My young, literal mind imaged a formal introduction of the two. Did they shake hands or what?

For the most part, as I grew older the lessons and experiences with the sacrament of extreme unction only added to my first innocent impression that the hour of death was the time for this last-ditch effort to clean up your act. It seemed like a cold and lonely means of grace.

Thank God, Vatican Council II returned the sacrament to the scriptural concept of healing. In its implementation in 1974, it was named the "sacrament of the sick." The reform avoided the term "last rites" and opened the rite to go beyond the actual anointing to include the ministry of the sick.

Some years ago, prior to a serious operation, I received the sacrament of the sick. I was not in danger of death, but fear had been crouching on the edge of my consciousness for over a week. I did not speak of it, for to name it would release it to infect those dearest to me. I smiled as I bustled about getting things in order and looking for a flattering robe for convalescence. To the observer I was optimistic and positive.

One day I thought, "You're a pretty good actress, but the Lord doesn't hand out Academy Awards. Don't be phony with him." I visited my pastor. Because I had dallied so long, there was no time to involve the family. As he anointed my forehead and hands, a sense of holy peace replaced the fear wasting my energies. It didn't change my clutching at life, but I felt my own identity merging with Christ's passion over the hopeless, the frightened, and the lonely. I had a new perspective on my life with all its fragility and strength.

After the operation, my sense of oneness with Jesus must have been apparent, for the chaplain brought to my room several persons who were combating the fear I had faced. We talked and prayed together. Since then my compassion and empathy with those who are ill, in body or spirit, has become an active part of my ministry. I often think how much more health-giving the sacrament of the sick is today. Also, I think that the meeting with God is not a formal handshake but an embrace.

People should seek the sacrament more often. It helps. Bill had successful bypass surgery, but his recuperation was a period of dark shadows and alienation. He said, "I began to hate my body for its unceasing demand for rest and my preoccupation with the functioning of my organs. My focus was inward. It was a struggle to talk to my family and friends. Sometimes I didn't bother. Prayer? My interior silence was simply that: silent. God had found another sanctuary. I was so filled with myself, there was no room for him. I discovered what hell means.

"My son Tom stood by and watched my agony just so long. Then he gently moved in, but armed for battle. I knew my stubbornness was no match for his persistence, so I agreed to see our parish priest. He came. I talked, he listened. He understood my depression. He asked if I wished to receive the sacrament of the sick, for while my body was working itself back to health, my spirit was receiving no healing in its illness. Father said that the purpose of the sacrament is to restore the wholeness of the person. I agreed to it.

"The family and my closest friends came to pray with Father Ben. It was like one of the children's baptisms—a time of celebration and a consciousness of the relationship of our humanity with the passion, death, and Resurrection of Christ. Slowly, with the help I finally accepted, I came out of myself. Today, two years later, I help Father with others who are living a similar experience and at parish communal rites for the sick. I'm proof that God mends all kinds of brokenness."

The Cross We Carry

*"When sorrows come, they come not single spies,
but in battalions."*

The winds of the Great Depression scattered my family's resources but not our resourcefulness, our hope, or our faith. My
parents prophesied, "Things will get better, but in the meantime
. . ." In the meantime my mother pressed my father's suit daily so
that he could greet the world undaunted. The suit came to have a
life of its own as it traveled on the backs of neighbors going for
their job interviews.

We went without, but we did not go hungry. We pulled
strength from each other, knew joys and laughter, and prayed a
good deal. My mother, who wore her galoshes and winter coat in
the house before stoking the furnace when we came home from
school, often reminded us: "God helps those who help themselves.
He will not forget us." Things did get better. The best is that my
brother and I today know how to cope with life's adversities. I
have two other stories of "carrying one's cross" and creating new
life out of it.

Tom has the swagger of the locker-room champ. A successful
salesman, he is good company at social functions except when he
indulges his passion for reciting sports statistics.

I met his son, Mike, at a summer party. A string bean of a
youth, he struggled to keep his awkwardness under control and
hide behind his National Honor Society achievement, knowing he
never would be the football star that his father would have liked
to see. Mike hopes to become a psychologist and "make people's
lives easier and more loving." He added, "My dad is good at slapping your back, but he can't hug anyone, even my mom."

19

Sally, Tom's wife, is not the typical wife of a cold and domineering husband. Self-assured, with a quick sense of humor, she wryly unraveled her story: "I could take his persistent crowding of me with his orders, even ignore some, but his coldness was a catheter inserted into my spirit, draining out my sense of sexuality. I felt drably undesirable. Then, about ten years ago, I said to myself, 'This is craziness. Tom refuses therapy. If I stay with him, I'll have to be my own ego booster.' Mike and I saw a counselor. I stopped stuffing myself with food and went back to work. I am now a supervising nurse. Our marriage isn't perfect, but what is? Tom is a good man. He's not mean. He just can't break out of the person his strict, undemonstrative father and he created. He needs support too, but he just can't ask for it. I am glad that Mike will not hand on his cycle."

Twenty-two years ago I first met Harvey, a vigorous sixty-year-old teacher of English in a public school. He shone with the gentleness of one who has wrestled with life. Born into the decay of the ghetto, he knew his students' struggles. Harvey had suffered with dignity the slights of the white academic community and savored the sweet victory of acceptance for himself and other black educators. Through the years of pain he remained philosophical and persevering, often quoting the line from Hamlet, "When sorrows come, they come not single spies, but in battalions."

We visited recently in his retirement home in northern Florida. His shift in attitude upset me. He quietly mused: "I now realize that by moving to another city to be near my niece I have chopped away my roots, the familiar streets and people who gave me life. I have become the dry stick I never thought I would become. Everything seems like a cold winter day, especially the last hours when the gray settles down and darkness comes too soon. The people here are nice, but they are strangers, except for Sister Anne. Can you imagine, she's trying to convince me to lead a discussion group on books? It's nonsense. No one will be interested."

I encouraged him to try, reminding him of his past successes. I have since heard from him: "It was slow at first, but more and more people came, and we have a group of about fifteen. They're lonely folks just like me. Life is not so wintry-dark anymore, and I think this transplanted stick is beginning to root again."

Being Who God Intends Us to Be

*The art of living successfully is learned slowly
from lessons in bits and snatches.*

I was dozing on the sofa when I became conscious of my father speaking to my mother in a voice unlike his own. He sounded sad, mad, and tired at the same time. "Al is in real trouble. He's taking bribes and running around on Agnes. He won't listen to me. He's getting away with it now, but I told him living a lie only leads to disaster."

I pretended to sleep as they talked softly about their friends. I was frightened for Al and Agnes and their children. I also had a sensation of great distrust for my own future. I was ten years old. Their family seemed very nice. Their house was grander than ours. Their car bigger. Nothing fit. How would I be when I grew up?

It troubled me so much that eventually I talked to my mother about it. She made no comment about my eavesdropping but counseled me: "Not every life is what it seems. Success in the world doesn't always mean you are successful. Greed and pride often lead to dishonesty, which captures you like a fly in a web. The important thing is that you are true to yourself and what you know is good. That's all God asks. And he is the one you must answer to."

Eventually, Al lost his job as a buyer for a big company. Jobs were scarce after the Great Depression, and his guilt was bigger than his capacity to come back. His girlfriend moved on when the champagne stopped flowing. Agnes remained faithful, as did my parents. I have recollections of many trips made by my father to jail or flophouses to bring Al home. The last call was that he was DOA at the city hospital. In the eyes of the world, Al was a failure. At the funeral, my mother said gently: "It's not for us to judge. Only God knows what made Al do what he did."

The art of living successfully is learned slowly from lessons in bits and snatches. Hopefully we grow stronger and wiser with age. However, some people fall into a routine of mistakes and repeat them over and over. I have an acquaintance who seemed to live without a compass and invariably take the wrong turn. Stella married Hank after a whirlwind romance that knocked her off balance. For a couple of years she rode an emotional teeter-totter until she and Hank decided to divorce. It was amiable and a relief, but Stella was warped by what she thought was her failure to make the blighted promise of the marriage work. Her image of herself was an impediment to future relationships, and she repeatedly found herself at dead ends.

After much urging from her family, she attended a meeting of the parish's support group for divorced persons. She did not return; she said she wasn't ready. It was more pleasant to hear hollow compliments and live in a feelingless void than to face the truth about herself.

Recently she related to me what she called her "shining moment": "I had agreed to meet this new man. I walked into the bar crowded with noisy people who seemed no more human than sea gulls shrieking and flapping over morsels on the beach. The air hung heavy with perfume, smoke, and stale alcohol. I stood at the entrance and asked myself, 'How have I let myself come to this?' For reasons I could not sort, I wanted to get out and be quiet. I went home and let the tears come. They were different— like a cleansing spring rain preparing the ground for new growth. It's a time I will never forget, for it was my turning point."

I don't suppose most of us become all we have dreamed of being. Often we have the insight that some things are not for us anyway. Success, in the long run, is being the person God intended us to be. That's a lifelong challenge.

Leaning with Each Other

*"When the first green shoots sprouted like a pale green sea
on our cleared land, Bob and I knew we had become
a real part of the caring community we sought."*

Interdependence is a new term for the age-old complex pattern of dependency and mutual responsibility. It's a functional term, but it pales in comparison with the blazing vision of the loving community Christ showed us in becoming one with us.

Children learn early to receive, but they need to be taught how to be responsible, generous, and loving givers. Otherwise they grow in the self-absorbed delusion that everything they wish is for their taking.

I remember Saturday mornings: I was moving slowly down the street with Mrs. Rosenthal leaning on me. I was about nine years old and not very tall, but the two black babushkas on our heads were almost at the same height. The weight of her years had squashed her frail bones into the high shoes she wore under her long, black skirt. It was a wobbly trip of a block-and-a-half to the synagogue. Mrs. Rosenthal lived next door to us. She was an Orthodox Jew, as were her family who lived elsewhere. In observance of the Sabbath none of them could ride in a car. She was the only Jew on our street; the rest of the Jewish community lived on the other side of the synagogue.

When my mother suggested that I accompany Mrs. Rosenthal to her place of worship, I did not think it strange that I would attend a Jewish service on Saturday and a Catholic Mass on Sunday. I ran many errands for Mrs. Rosenthal as part of what my mother called "helping each other." In fact, I felt pretty important being chosen for this responsibility.

I enjoyed the voice of the cantor at the temple, although I did not understand him, nor could I respond when the people spoke to me in Yiddish. But I could tell by their smiles that they liked me. Sitting quietly in the back pew, I had a taste of the God-mystery and the reverence of people other than those in my parish church. It strengthened me to ignore the ugly taunts of the neighborhood kids who were mimicking the prejudices of their parents. The memory still sustains me today whenever someone tries to slice away at a portion of the human race because they are

different. As in most human transactions, I was both a giver and a receiver, and I am grateful for the blessing of knowing what I have received.

Acts of interdependence have a way of feeding more interdependence. Bob is a pharmacist, and Nan is a nurse who grew up with my children. They both had bright futures in a metropolitan hospital. Yet they decided to work in a clinic in a smaller city, for much less money. Nan explained: "We began to feel we had lost our identities in that huge hospital, and we were stifled in our apartment complex with its anonymous closed doors. We wanted to have the time to be closer to our patients. We needed space to walk, to marvel at the stars, to smell the sweet air of the changing seasons. We bought a small farm. We had no intentions of working the land, but hoped that it would be a good and healthy community for the family we hope to have.

"Our closest neighbors are directly across the gravel road. Neither of us had much front yard so it was easy to get acquainted. Frank and Liz are hardworking, good people, third-generation farmers who have degrees in agriculture from the state university. They are known for their fine kernel corn, glossy white eggplants, and many other advanced vegetables. Through the summer, fall, and winter there was some time for the four of us to share dreams. Bob and I came to realize that for Frank and Liz, the land was a sacred trust. It was no surprise then when they asked to rent all or part of our fifteen acres.

"Bob and I talked about it and thought such an arrangement would not tamper with our reasons for moving to the farm. As we talked we began to see our responsibility to the land and community. We made the following proposal: We would lend them the land to plant what they thought best in this soil that had been dormant for several seasons. We asked that one-third of the harvest go to the soup kitchen in town where we worked as volunteers. We would take what we needed for our table, and the rest would be theirs to sell. After all, it was their labor and their gamble. Frank and Liz agreed. When the first green shoots sprouted like a pale green sea on our cleared land, Bob and I knew we had become a real part of the caring community we sought."

Unveiling Beauty

"You have been blessed with many talents;
not the least of them is the creation of beauty."

In my junior year in high school, I had a great teacher of English, Sister Angela Marie, OP. I admired her and loved her classes. I painted large illustrations of the literature we were studying for the walls of her classroom. There was an empathy between us.

After school one day she took me aside to talk. With the prophetic air of a new Moses, she proclaimed: "You have been blessed with many talents; not the least of them is the creation of beauty. If you do not use all of them to bring others to God, you will be doomed to hell." Strong stuff for a sixteen-year-old, but Sister was the type you "Yes, sistered" when she was serious. The conversation ended and was never referred to again.

Sister's message was almost too powerful to bear, but intuitively I knew she was right, even if I didn't quite understand it. I have never forgotten it. It has set the direction of my life. With the years, its wisdom and truth have continually evolved. In the process, I have also learned which gift or gifts God is calling forth at a particular time.

With this background, I was delighted to be assisting my stepdaughter, Elaine, to exhibit her fine-art calligraphy at the prestigious, international Art Expo/New York at the Javits Convention Center. A hundred thousand people visited the show, one of the largest in the world.

It was our first experience at such a show, but a gratifying one. Thousands of persons passing our small booth affirmed us by smiling with spontaneous pleasure at seeing her beautiful and unique work.

Also, it was a learning experience. We were plunged into the enormous variety of art and artists. The first two days of the exhibit were reserved exclusively for tradespeople, those urbane dealers in art who are not only interested in beauty but in beauty that will be purchased for galleries or produced in limited editions and unlimited editions or posters—a form of sharing beauty at a lower cost since the time of the French Impressionists. We dealt with the trade representatives cautiously, but we were grateful that people around the world would know the beauty of Elaine's work.

On the third day, the trade specialists were still reviewing and establishing their choices, but members of the general public came streaming through. Most of them had traveled into New York by train and paid a ten-dollar admission fee to the show.

One visitor was a small, modest woman with a tired face. She appreciated Elaine's work and asked for a catalog. We had reserved them for the tradespeople and the private collectors. Then we heard Helen's story. She taught in an inner-city school in New Jersey. As she spoke, her inner beauty transformed her plainness into the kind of radiance shown in religious paintings in the middle ages.

Helen's mission was to give her sixth-grade students precious experiences of beautiful art so that these memories would flow through their consciousness like an underground stream: fresh, sparkling, refreshing. Hopefully it would be a lifetime source of comfort and joy. She shook her head as she said, "My students live surrounded by graffiti, dirt, broken bottles, and broken lives. It should not be this way. I really believe God meant the gift of beauty for every human being: to be beautiful, to see beauty, to share beauty, and to create beauty. Ugliness is the dark side of beauty. It is the curse of man's inhumanity to man."

Her stubborn persistence rubbed away any resistance the students had to looking at art reproductions, discussing them, and writing essays about what they had experienced. Her voice became more animated as she related her recent success: "I proposed to the class that we hire a bus and visit the Metropolitan Museum of Art in New York City. We enthusiastically discussed the project. Realistically, our biggest obstacle was financing. The students volunteered to get family recipes and publish a cookbook to raise money.

"The students showed remarkable ingenuity. They owned the project. They made the money. They paid for the bus and the box lunches. Permission was received from the school for a release day; the museum waived the admission fees and provided a guide.

"At the museum, the students—in the presence of the original pieces of art—stood absorbed by what they saw. Even I was surprised by their quiet, almost reverential awe. They whispered to each other but had many questions for the guide about the art and the artists.

"On the bus returning home we talked about what we saw, what we liked, how we felt. Melinda, usually shy, spoke up, 'I feel different, kinda like I'm more beautiful inside. I'm glad we did this!' Several students 'yeah-yeahed' Tony when he commented that most of the artists had been poor like us. 'Maybe some of us can be artists too, good artists that make things beautiful. Not trashy stuff like we see around us!' Frightened little Tillie whispered, 'That man, van Gogh, talked to me.' She said, 'I know.'"

We gave Helen the brochure with the promise of sending her more examples of the art we have in our collections. We wanted to be part of her legacy of beauty.

God has given us boundless beauty in nature and unnumbered gifted, creative persons. Beauty sneaks up on us in the unveiling of a person, touches us in a film, strokes us in a novel, envelopes us in an art piece. Can the forces of destruction stop it? Never, unless they destroy life itself.

Our Own Special Pilgrimage

Each of our personal pilgrimages through life
is wonderfully a paradox: unimaginably separate and unique,
but connected to each person who moves in and out of our life
and is a part of the events that shape us.

There was a little girl who believed in a secret world existing under the stairway in her grandmother's house. There was a woman who believed in it too—or so she said she did—and the two spun secret stories of the wonders behind the wall.

They grew together, nourishing each other like silence and sound. The woman's journey-map was confined to caring for the family's sick and elderly, to her daily trip to the parish church for Mass, and to fifty years of being the guardian of the altars and linens. The girl matured, embracing with exhilaration the freshness of life. She traveled to unknown places, met the powerful and the poor. Her life was brimming full.

The woman entered into the girl's adventures with a delighted ear and gave gifts of what she would have relished had her life been different: exotic perfumes, white kid gloves, and lace handkerchiefs.

The years began to weigh heavily on the tiny, spunky woman. After her eightieth birthday and for the next few years, the girl—now, certainly, a woman herself—became the caretaker of the older woman. They spent much time together, laughing and remembering, like rolling over old stones to discover some hidden treasure. In the looking backward, God's name frequently came up. God's goodness, love, and care served as reference points of happenings they shared. The two were celebrating what the poet Jessica Powers said: "Heaven is something happening in the soul."

When the woman died, a part of me joined her, for she—my aunt, godmother and friend—connected me with who I had been, and therefore with who I am. Yet our relationship is not exhausted. It goes on singing in my heart.

Each of our personal pilgrimages through life is wonderfully a paradox: unimaginably separate and unique, but connected to each person who moves in and out of our life and is a part of the events that shape us.

There is a universality of struggle and pain in trying to penetrate our personal mystery. Sometimes we are rewarded by others, sometimes it is a lonely quest. Perhaps one of the reasons reunions are so popular is that they bring us to those who remember us. We hope we may be able to touch again that moment that explains life's later decisions. It could have been the nudging support of a teacher who saw a light in us we had not yet set spark. Someone may help us perceive a pattern still with us today: a healthy respect for each human being because of the open heart and pocketbook of a parent, or an unfortunate nagging prejudice that had burst open at a school competition and still itches under our skin.

Occasionally reviewing our personal pilgrimage helps us move into a mature way of being ourselves. If we don't retell our story (even to ourselves), we could suffer a kind of amnesia that closes off the growth that we are called to seek. At the same time, forever glancing over our shoulders or hiding inside our albums or journals is not growing either. That borders on the dangerous and, at the least, is boring, especially to those around us. Life's pilgrimage should be forward. Remembering simply shows us where we have been, how unique we are, so we can walk with greater strength into the future.

Happy are those who walk with those who share a common belief: that somehow, no matter what our talents, who we are, or where we journey, we are, as Pope John Paul II said in his first encyclical, *Redemptor Hominis,* the way the church fulfills its mission . . . "the prophetic mission that comes from Christ himself."

We used to use the term *pilgrimage* in the context of a prayerful visit to a sacred site or shrine like the Holy Land or

Lourdes. Since Vatican Council II, we speak of all Christians as being on pilgrimage: seeing Christ in each other and being Christ for
each other. Pilgrimage then is ongoing, like maturing, a movement
forward with less earthly baggage and a greater fullness of the
spirit. Our singular, unique, and unrepeatable pilgrimage is all of
our days strung together: dawns and sunsets, fogs and storms, still
pools and many, many persons.

The more people we touch, either personally or through our
talents, the more our story is retold. If our touch is for good, the
story retells it, just as I told my of Aunt Edna's. It continues, we
continue. There is no end as long as there is someone who re-
members and tells another. In a real way our individual pilgrimage
is never over until all pilgrims are home.

Even God Took a Day Off

*I doubt that Gramma knew much about Saint Teresa of Ávila,
but she would have understood her statement, "Letting go
proceeds from the center of the soul and awakens the person
to a new consciousness and a new compassion."*

I was about twelve when I spent a summer month visiting my friend Rosemary's grandmother. Gramma Gannon, a tiny, wise, Irish dynamo who had raised thirteen children, lived in farm country, high on a hill overlooking a small town in Ontario.

Gramma had definite ideas about life and blessed our young lives with the opportunity to experience the deep truths she had learned. Rosemary and I observed the routine of the house. We rose early, doggedly attacked the weeds in Gramma's vegetable patch, and fed the chickens. Then we were free to rush down the hill to plunge our sweaty bodies into the cool waters of the rock quarry.

By noon we were ready for Aunt Margaret's main meal of the day: plates filled with boiled beef or chicken, onions, potatoes, fresh vegetables, and homemade bread.

Once the kitchen was clean, Gramma Gannon would move into her rocking chair, throw her apron up from her waist over her face, and "settle in for a wee bit." When her fingers stopped moving on her rosary and the white cloth of her apron puffed up and down with her deep breathing, we knew she was asleep.

Our chance for escape? We were expected to "settle in" also, to doze or to read the books we had brought from home. We grumbled, but Aunt Margaret was a stern enforcer. So we complied and soon looked forward to the respite.

Reading had always been a great joy to me, but on many days the book rested unopened on the swing next to me. I entered into the dreamy world of the senses: the heady scent of the climbing roses and honeysuckle whose tangled branches created an intimate bower of the small front porch. Only the hum of insects and the creak of the swing broke the silence. I would stare into the mists rising from the river in the valley that quickly dropped on the other side of the dirt road in front of the house. The mists were like the mystery of God.

I gave myself over to nature and let it speak to me. A child of the city, I was learning insights into quiet, letting go, and getting in touch with myself, and—maybe—God.

After an hour or so, Gramma's chair would rock. She would smooth down her apron on her lap, blink her bright blue eyes, and ask, "Are the likes of you ready for a game of Parcheesi?" I doubt that Gramma knew much about Saint Teresa of Ávila, but she would have understood her statement, "Letting go proceeds from the center of the soul and awakens the person to a new consciousness and a new compassion."

Gramma's lessons were far-reaching. When my children were small, our pattern in the summer was to straighten the house and then take off for a two-hour walk along Lake Huron. They were more like expeditions into strange lands because the beach changed daily. Fueled by children's avid curiosities, we paused to watch tadpoles or a sleepy turtle on the edge of the canal. We picked up quartz-filled stones glistening in the sun and shells as tiny as a baby's fingernail.

Back home, our pails were always full of treasures, our stomachs hungry, our bodies tired. After lunch we all "settled in": the littlest ones to nap, the older ones to read or look at books, to draw or to dream.

The rule was to have a time apart, to be content with themselves, and to enjoy the quiet. There was little rebellion, for it was the pattern that they had always known each summer. Now that they have grown and are parents themselves, they still respect and are nourished by nature and prize periods of play, quiet, rest, and solitude. They all have demanding careers to juggle with family responsibilities, but the roots of their youthful experiences have produced healthy adult habits.

With their families they still walk the beaches, hike in the woods, sail, wind surf, get up at dawn to photograph the sunrise, ride in the country to see fall's spectacular adieu to summer, walk gently in the spring to catch a glimpse of white trilliums and golden marsh marigolds. They also visit art and science museums and attend music performances, the theater, sports events, and any number of other activities.

In the school year the rhythm of their days is adjusted to the interests and events of their children: the sports of the season, performances in plays, choirs, and scholastic competitions. They are busy, yes. Stressed out? Not too often.

When I question them, I receive a variety of answers: "My body tells me what I can do and not do." "Living as we do is part of our family value system." "Sure, we get tired, but it's a normal, healthy tiredness." "It makes life more interesting—work alone could become an obsession or boring." "God has given us many wonders to enjoy. We take advantage of his generosity." "It brings peace out of what could be chaos."

What do they give up? Television is not their constant companion. They are social beings without excessive partying, and bar-hopping is not on their agendas.

My friend Betsy, a hair stylist, gave an interesting answer when I asked what she did to rest. Her reply indicated a person who knew herself and her needs. "All day long I give myself away. In order to own myself at the end of the day, I have a morning ritual. I arise earlier than would be normally needed and leisurely get myself mentally, physically, and emotionally focused and organized. I anticipate my day; I set goals. Otherwise, the pressure of time, fatigue from the fast pace, and the unpleasant attitude of a few clients can put me just inches from tears or an impatient grumpiness. When it happens I don't like myself. Also, my husband and I escape for a weekend at a resort now and then. We leave worries and annoyances behind. We get our marbles together—otherwise they're all scattered, and so is our life. After the weekend we return to the old routine of work, refreshed and stronger."

Rest is re-creative, active not passive. It doesn't just happen. It must be purposely planned. It frees our spirits to be open to the Spirit. Without rest we can never have the fullness of life that Jesus promised us.

Everyday Christmas

We celebrate the birthday of Jesus each year at Christmas,
but it is the adult Jesus who is with us, helping us find the way.

Since childhood I have experienced warm and wonderful memories of Christmas celebrated with dear familiar faces and rituals in my parish church, where the people, the hymns, and the joy-filled bells fit into a pattern like a jigsaw puzzle without any missing parts. This Christmas image has insulated me from realizing the awesome extent of what the birth of the Son of God means to me and all humanity.

The Christmas Eve of 1944 brought me into a set of circumstances that expanded my understanding of transformation. They led me to sit awhile with Mary, the expectant mother of Jesus—as one young woman to another—to learn something of the secret of Christmas and her courage to do God's work.

Nations were clutched in the horror of World War II. I was a new bride with a child beginning to form within me, a captive of nausea, fear, and loneliness in a strange room in a boardinghouse in Louisiana. There was no space for married officers at the army base, and the townspeople did not look kindly on Catholics, but we were fortunate that I did not need to go home, as some wives were forced to do.

My husband, Gene, had completed his Army Air Corp tour of duty in Europe and was assigned to flight instruction at an air base nearby. On this Christmas Eve, he was grounded by fog in Saint Louis, and our chances of being together for our first Christmas were meager.

On that dreary afternoon I looked at the tiny figures in the manger my parents had sent us and thought about how Mary must have felt far away from her home when she was ready to give birth. It struck me as symbolic of her that after the angel Gabriel had told her that God wanted her to bring the savior into the world, and she had accepted so graciously, she rushed off to be with Elizabeth, her kinswoman. Elizabeth needed her because she was elderly and six months pregnant with John. Mary wasn't concerned about herself. She didn't ask unnecessary questions; she simply went to be of help and to bring the unborn Jesus to Elizabeth and John.

Now, after the bumpy, exhausting journey on the small beast over the rocky terrain, Mary's hour was at hand, and there was no kinswoman to help her. She had no privacy, no space but what

Joseph cleared for her in pushing aside the cattle dung and straw in the stable. Out of her faith and courage, from her flesh came Jesus. He became present to her, but did she realize he became present to every human being?

That's what I was missing in my listless preoccupation with myself. Jesus was alive for me, and since I knew this, I needed to see that he became alive for others at this time, for all the strangers who lived in this house.

I had a box of cookies, candies, and some wine that had been sent to us. It was enough for a celebration of strangers! I spoke to my kind landlady, Mrs. Rich, about inviting the other boarders in for the evening. Gene's and my room had originally been the old house's living room, so it was larger than the others. Mrs. Rich agreed to bring glasses and napkins. I tacked an invitation on the house bulletin board.

Lily came first. A young woman from the mountains of Kentucky, she had a guitar and said she could play a few Christmas tunes. Old Mr. Schroeder stood at the edge of the door, timid and wary. He had been born and raised in Germany and carried the guilt of the war on his stooped shoulders. We asked him in, and he had with him a cardboard box covered with a yellowed newspaper. Inside was a beautiful collection of hand-blown ornaments, including a glistening star "from the old days," he said. There were tears in his eyes as he gave them to me. "Keep them, they were meant to be enjoyed."

The two "maiden ladies" arrived, smelling of lavender and moth balls, in dresses that rustled as they helped decorate the tree that Gene and I had bought before he left. Mrs. Rich produced the fruitcake she was "saving for company," and Mr. Rich came with a quart jar of a suspicious liquid that burned as it trickled down your throat. The tree was decorated. We sang Christmas hymns to a country tempo and toasted each other and the season with a new fondness. Jesus was alive among us!

It is not a romantic notion that the spirit of Christmas can move even a Scrooge to compassion and community. We celebrate the birthday of Jesus each year at Christmas, but it is the adult Jesus who is with us, helping us find the way.

Weeping Alone over Life's Losses

*"With God's help I can properly battle life's problems.
I'm a different, stronger person, and I know
you're never as alone as you think."*

We can expect losses in our lives, but our reactions are not always predictable. Depending upon the magnitude of the losses and our own strength at the time, we deal with some, but others remain on the smudged edges of our lives, hurting on and off to the rhythm of our vulnerability. Death, divorce, and the finality of terminal illness rally the community's grief but, with some losses, we weep alone.

Denise and Virginia were successful in their banking careers. I frequently saw them together at civic and professional meetings. Then I began to see Virginia alone and asked her if her friend had moved away. Virginia answered, "Moved on." Her eyes told me this was not easy to accept. I mumbled something inadequate like "That's too bad."

Virginia asked if I would like a coffee. We skipped the rest of the lecture and talked in the hotel coffee shop. We worked on a couple of Catholic Charity boards together, so we were more than acquaintances. Virginia related the story of the loss of her friend. "After I became close to Denise, I realized she had been a drifter, moving from person to person, telling her story over and over, changing friends, jobs, apartments, and even husbands. I thought our relationship of four years had finally broken the cycle. Denise said she felt she had at last found a true friend."

"We had so much in common: our interest in finance, the shared challenge of being women in the male-dominated world, even reaching forty in the same year! She told me so much about herself, I felt sorry and protective. We saw each other several times a week, and she was included in my family celebrations. We were good friends, yet we did not absorb each other's lives.

"Suddenly, six months ago, Denise told me she had asked to be transferred to the mortgage department that is located in another building. She was evasive about setting a lunch date in the future with the excuse of being immersed in her new responsibilities. I bided my time, but I was hurt. Her rejection created an invisible wound that continued to weep. I had a number of conversations with God, hoping that I would be able to forgive the fickleness of my friend just as he had.

"I called her a couple of times. She was busy, enthused about her new job, excited about her new coworkers. The conversations were bright as ice. Her tone buried the ghosts of our numberless personal conversations. I thought it was over. It wasn't that easy. We met last week at a corporation party. I tried to appear nonchalant, but I was crackling with the lightening of anger that had no place to go but tear through me. It was pointless to direct it at her. I guess the anger was a normal reaction. In a way, it was cleansing. That evening I decided I would let go. I miss her, but I understand the journey of a loner. They travel light."

Brian suffered a different loss, but his solitariness was similar. He said, "At first, I wanted to be quiet and alone. I needed time to put myself together, but relatives thought I had given up and started moving in on me.

"I had lost my job as an electrical engineer when my company merged. After looking for three months I was still unemployed. Marion, my wife, had found a full-time secretarial position, and I became the caretaker of the three kids and the house. I wasn't very good at it; I was so preoccupied and scared. Marion was wonderfully understanding, but her family did not share her belief in me. Their accusations of giving up and being lazy were shattering the spirit I had left. Marion encouraged me to go back to college for retraining. My previous education and experience proved to be a great foundation for the new field of data processing repair. I now have a job with a solid future, for I am employed by one of the largest corporations. I choose to let the year fold back on itself like it never happened, except for two things: Marion's belief in me, and what I learned about myself—that with God's help I can properly battle life's problems. I'm a different, stronger person, and I know you're never as alone as you think."

People with a Mission

Susan and Steve, who refused to be shackled by their ordinariness, have achieved a grandeur few can match, none can buy.

Susan was thirty-seven when she began to study nursing. She left her beloved husband to live in a room in our neighborhood. It was a short walk to the hospital that had awarded her a study grant. Her husband, Steve, remained in a small town halfway across the country, perfecting his skill with engines: car, truck, farm equipment—any kind. He was considered a legend of sorts in the community because of his ability to fix anything with moving parts. Unfortunately, his income was not equal to his reputation.

During the two years they lived apart, they wrote each other daily, spacing their phone calls to once a month. She journeyed home only for Christmas. To many people their life seemed strange, almost harsh, until you understood that their rare generosity of spirit was fueled by their dream—to become missionaries.

Susan's basic practicality led her to study nursing. She explained to me: "Steve and I are just ordinary people. We've done nothing special with our lives, but we know God's people need help. It's up to us to be the best we can be. Steve is a natural fixer, and I think I'm a healer. But I need to be able to do more than hold a suffering person's hand."

Prior to her community college courses, Susan's education had been sketchy. So it was necessary for her to immerse herself in study. To save money, she ate her meals at the hospital, but she was spartan about hospital social activities. In the beginning, her younger classmates dismissed her as a fanatic, but as they came into closer contact, her sweetness of spirit drew them to her. The students caught themselves, sometimes by surprise, tutoring her before tests in subjects in which she was weak. However, on the floor with the patients, it was their turn to observe. Susan's compassion and selflessness tucked the ill into blankets of security and hope. She had the capacity of emptying herself to totally concentrate on the patient.

As soon as Susan graduated, she returned to Steve. They sold their home and possessions. Sixteen years ago, they went to remote islands of the South Pacific to work with various religious orders as well as the Peace Corps. Their Christmas card this year was from Fiji.

They are still serving. Susan's life is a love song to her husband as well as her God. Four years ago, Steve was incapacitated by a stroke that robbed him of his gift to repair the broken-down, chugging, hissing motors. He is confined to a wheelchair but accompanies Susan on her rounds. She writes: "Steve has regained his speech, if not the use of his hands. While he does not do the same work as he did, he is a wonderful listener and is surrounded by the people wherever I work. Sometimes, the elders invite him to their meetings. We are fine. This is where we were meant to be."

Their dream has been realized. They have brought Jesus to thousands of people. Susan and Steve, who refused to be shackled by their ordinariness, have achieved a grandeur few can match, none can buy.

Being Christian Love

Our young family learned that love and trust are enormous
mysteries to anyone who has almost never known them.

She stood on the porch one day this summer, close to the door, a stout black woman. A tall, gray-haired man stood directly behind her, and two children, a boy and a girl, held her hands. Her broad smile indicated that she expected to be welcomed like a relative returning from a trip. I waited until she said, "Mom, you haven't changed very much except for the white in your hair."

Twenty some years disappeared, and I blurted out, "Marilyn!" We embraced with laughter and tears and, as she introduced her husband and grandchildren, she kept saying, "I told you she would remember me, even if I did get fat!"

Marilyn was eighteen and had just graduated from high school when she left us to go south for a job with some cousins in Georgia. She promised to call upon her arrival, and she did. We exchanged some letters until ours came back "address unknown." Our efforts to find her were fruitless.

Marilyn had been in a class taught by my Aunt Ruth. She was a fifteen-year-old whose life had been a joyless stretch of neglect and abuse. My aunt saw that this bright girl would be systematically destroyed if she were not whisked out of her world into one of trust and love. Ruth prevailed upon us to take Marilyn in and raise her with the six children we had then.

It was a gamble, but we took the risk. Marilyn was not the first of the troubled girls who stayed with us for a year or so.

I look back now and wonder how we managed. I guess we accepted Marilyn as part of the whole strong song of love that kept on singing in our lives in spite of our frayed nerves and frustration and her early resistance to just about everything from food to curfews.

Our young family learned that love and trust are enormous mysteries to anyone who has almost never known them. These mysteries must be seen as well as felt. We became more conscious of our relationships with each other. My husband and I saw that what we were trying to do carried a crucial message about our relationship with God, for in our loving we were echoing God's love for us.

When we no longer heard from Marilyn, we wondered what more we could have done in preparing her for a life of her own. Now she was back, bubbling like a fountain, pouring forth her history of a stable, caring family with modest financial success and a dedication and involvement in the church. "Just like you, Mom," she proudly explained. She and Tom, her husband, had converted to Catholicism when they were first married. They raised five children and had several grandchildren.

Marilyn, Tom, and the two grandchildren were on a trip to northern Michigan from their home outside Atlanta. Marilyn had convinced Tom to take a detour so that she could return to where she had spent summers on Lake Huron. She must have locked a picture of the house and grounds in her memory, for she guided her family on a tour of every nook and cranny, with special emphasis on the room that had been hers. She told stories to her grandchildren about her "brothers and sisters," even Therese who was not yet born when she left and known only through the early letters.

She wanted to know about my husband, "Dad," and the grandparents—all of whom had died. She grew very quiet and then said with genuine conviction, "I'm sure they are all in heaven. They were so good to me."

I wanted Marilyn, Tom, and the kids to stay, but their plan was to go to Copper Harbor and be back as scheduled to Tom's printing business.

Upon leaving, Tom declared, "She's a wonderful, good, and loving woman, and I bless you for all you did for her."

Marilyn lingered a bit as the others reached the car. "You all were a puzzlement to me at first, but I caught on that you were with me all the way. I was important to someone for the first time. I learned about the best things in life from you. Whenever folks talk about home, I tell about my three years with you. It's really when my life began. The rest, before—well it was such a mess, it's almost forgotten."

Recently I asked a veteran religious educator how to teach Christian love. Her answer was, "You can't teach it, you have to *be* it." I understand.

A Lifestyle's Delicate Web

In today's usage, the definition of lifestyle leans toward possessions. I wish to emphasize attitudes and grace as factors in shaping lifestyles.

Most persons, in their journey from birth to death, bump against hundreds of situations that leave marks and shed bits of wisdom. These experiences influence us as we go forward and find our way back. The integration of our past, who we perceive ourselves to be, and present conditions shapes how we live the here-and-now in certain ways; this is what some call "lifestyle."

In today's usage, the definition of lifestyle leans toward possessions. I wish to emphasize attitudes and grace as factors in shaping lifestyles.

During the Great Depression, an elderly relative of my mother's, who had been reduced from a life of gracious gentility to being a boarder, came to stay in my mother's sewing room. She needed a place to live, and my parents could use the small amount that she could afford to pay. She moved through the house like a peevish gray storm-cloud, grumbling and muttering, refusing to acknowledge that we too had to compromise the way things used to be. She was oblivious to the absence of my mother's jewelry that shuttled between home and pawn shop. The jewelry became the barometer of our finances; when the wedding band went, our prayers doubled.

Depression days were universally hard to endure. The fates tested everyone and left them humiliated and despairing or toughened them with an abiding strength and dreams of good times just around the corner.

In our house the dreams were not totally dependent upon my father's talent or my mother's ingenuity. My parents were people of unflinching faith, and each crisis was allotted its own prayer. We prayed a lot.

When Bernadette arrived, she packed her hope and her good silk dress into her trunk. We never saw either one. As time went on, we saw less and less of her. She kept to her room, preparing her meals from our small supplies at odd times. After eating, she always had bicarbonate of soda behind the closed door to the basement. It released the gases of her stomach, but not the acid in her heart.

I ache for her today, but did little for her cantankerousness when I was a child. However, the mark she left on me helps me to be more sympathetic for those I meet today who are haunted by the angry ghosts of old hurts or who cannot face the reality of their present lives. Like Bernadette, they have trapped their smiles and their ability to cope in their musty trunk of yesteryear. Every so often someone's caring interest can work the miracle of rebirth for them. The long, empty life sheds its shell. The dormant seed opens but, fragile, it needs much nurturing. Jerry's was such a case.

Jerry was among the group sent into Hiroshima to clean up. He had left home with a nonchalant patriotic song and returned a broken record, repeating and repeating horror after horror. The government had provided psychiatric help, but unlike most of his buddies, he was released before he had healed. He came home to the small town of his roots, but only the local bar gave him short-term comfort.

Jerry's father had died while he was at war, and his mother grew into a strength of extraordinary proportions. The other children left one by one, but she persisted in caring for her son. One day, Jerry's army chaplain came and, after a week, Jerry returned to the hospital. A year later he was back with us. He would never be the carefree Jerry again, but the savage fires of his soul had been subdued. The townspeople relaxed and sighed when Jerry joined his mother at daily Mass and got a job on the newspaper.

After six months, he disappeared again. His mother kept the secret, saying only, "Jerry's fine and very happy." People surmised that he was somewhere building a new life. When his mother was dying, they knew that he had found a new life. Jerry returned in the robes of a monk, which he wore with peaceful serenity. His comments to his friends were simple. "At last I've found what I was born to do: console the victims of oppression and atone for the cruelty of war."

Friends

For a moment I was stunned by his emotion, but instinct or grace moved me to embrace him as I would a hurting child.

Some persons leave a mark on us even though they are part of our lives a brief time. We called them "friend" then. After they are gone, we still call them friend.

Joe was one of these. He delivered fresh vegetables and fruits on our street when my children were young. The crusty old man from southern Italy must have been a tough bargainer at the market in the gray-pink hours of dawn. Each of the baskets of produce in his converted station wagon invited touching with its ripe perfection, and the perfume brought a healthy, sensual joy at the miracle of nature.

Tough though Joe was, he needed a friend, and I became one for him. It was brief—June to October for five years—but it was no small relationship.

Joe's wife had died a few years before, and his only child, a daughter, had entered a cloistered convent when she was a very young woman. Most of his relatives were back in the "old country," as he called it. He lived in an ethnically mixed community in the inner city but somehow didn't fit in. In the wisdom of his years, he dulled his longing for the land by bringing the harvest of the land to others. It was also his livelihood.

He taught me how to select a melon and to keep tomatoes at room temperature so they would not lose their flavor. He introduced me into the exotic world of fresh herbs and inspired me with his profound reverence for garlic. I was an eager pupil, and my cooking has not been the same since.

On Thursdays, about mid-morning, he would be in our block. After the neighbors completed their purchases, he stopped into my sunny kitchen for coffee, extra strong and black. (Years later on my visits to Rome, I remembered Joe as I saw the men sipping their espresso at the tiny sidewalk tables in the golden light.)

If my children were around he would fill their imaginations with stories of his youth. When we were alone we talked about food, religion, and life. Joe had the simplicity of the truly good

person. He would never make history. To some he was an invisible servant, yet for others the tide of his life cleansed their fear and gave them an inner trust in the God they had lost in the scramble of living.

One day in the fifth year of our friendship, he seemed troubled. Ordinarily his deep eyes were calm. That day, as we sat at the kitchen table, they were like black stones shining from the bottom of a pool of water. Soon the tears flowed over, seeking the creases in his sun-weathered face and splashing down on his clean, blue shirt. Even though we were both nourished by our mutual fondness, there had never been any display of affection between us beyond a warm but dignified handshake when we parted. For a moment I was stunned by his emotion, but instinct or grace moved me to embrace him as I would a hurting child. The story came tumbling out.

In a rare letter, his beloved daughter had written that she had begun the process of leaving the convent. The orderliness of Joe's life was threatened. He had gladly given his only child to God. Now she was turning from God in what Joe saw as a blasphemous act of defiance of God's will. I tried to reassure him that such an action was allowable in the church and that, in fact, she might be responding to God's call for her at this time. Further, I felt that her decision had come after much prayer and counseling. I said, "She's a woman now, Joe. Tell her of your love and support. She needs it. It must be a hard time for her too." He relaxed and almost smiled, but withdrew inside himself. He finished his coffee and left—this time with an embrace.

For the rest of the summer and into October, he gave me reports of what meager news he received from his daughter. I suggested that he spend the winter near her in New York State if he could afford it.

In late spring, I received a note that began, "My dear friend." He indicated that he would stay in the East, selling produce and helping his daughter adjust. Two years later he wrote that God had blessed him with a beautiful granddaughter. There was never a return address on the envelopes, so I waited in silence.

A couple of years later a note came from his daughter. Joe had died while planting a garden for his granddaughter. She thanked me for being his friend.

Finding Our Way to God

I thought, "Ordinary?" His greatness shone through the transparency of his ordinariness.

Each of us must find our own way to God. We do it bit by bit, day by day. Each story, when it is retold, is different, with different metaphors describing each life of faith: seasons, journeys, weavings. While it will be our unique story, it will have been shaped by persons and events, hurts and joys. It will be our success story if we can say that we have become the kind of person God has called us to be. The story I will tell here is of John, whom I met when he was eighty-five years old.

The old man stood holding the church door open while the white-haired woman awkwardly slumping over her walker slowly moved up the handicap ramp. He beckoned to me to move around her. I said, "I can wait. I admire her courage."

He looked almost angrily at me and replied: "She doesn't have any courage. She doesn't know who she is. She's got Alzheimer's!" I softly said, "Bless you for having courage for both of you." Again the storm welled up in his eyes. "Somebody better bless us. God's forgotten us!"

I chose not to pursue it further. It was evident that his vulnerability had forced him into a hard-boiled self-protection. That he had made the considerable effort to get both of them to Mass said more about his faith in God than his words did.

By coincidence, a few days later I saw him in the supermarket parking lot. He was alone, cautiously inching across the patches of ice, clutching two grocery bags. I moved to help him. He recognized me, put one of his bags into my outstretched arms, and apologized for his harshness of Sunday.

We introduced ourselves, and John said, "It had been a hard morning. The winter of my life is like this day: dreary, dark, and chilling to my very soul. Everything seems to be disintegrating from what it used to be." His face was gentle now, and his voice was soft with wistful longing for what once was.

We had reached his car, but he continued to speak as if talking could help him discover some sunshine in the puzzling and painful situation in which he found himself. "Mary and I did everything together. We laughed a lot; she could always lighten my spirits. She never lost hope even when the Depression hit and we were just getting established. She had a beautiful love of the Blessed Mother, and we went to Our Lady of Perpetual Help devotions every Tuesday evening. In those days attendance at a novena was a satisfying outward sign of our growing trust and love of her son, Jesus.

"Somehow we got through the lean days, and our burdens became lighter. I moved up with each job change and eventually started my own plumbing business. We were never rich, but we put our four kids and two of my widowed sister's children through college.

"During the Korean War our oldest son, Tom, was in premedical school. He was called to service and went to Korea with the ambulance corps. Having our firstborn over there in that absurd war was a yoke that cut deeply. Even the Lord's promise, 'Come to me, all you who labor and are overburdened and I will give you rest,' did not sweeten my yoke. I gained my release in an occasional binge with the bottle. Mary continued to go about attending to things in our daily lives, but you could sense the heartache that haunted her. In the presence of Tom's danger, she gently drew our family to hold each other closer and turn more and more to God for courage.

"Previously, the kids would invent reasons to avoid saying the rosary together, but our common suffering helped them shed their youthful illusions that they were in control of their lives. They knew they had to turn to God.

"Tom was wounded and sent home. We all accepted our role of healing him in his body and spirit, which had been bent and torn by the repugnant scenes of war. Slowly our Tom came back to us. He has become a doctor who shows great compassion for his patients, especially those who are frightened.

"Someone said that suffering either breaks or strengthens you. The rough times and how we handled them forged our family bonds. We not only love each other, we enjoy being together. The sense of family closeness was absorbed by the grandchildren, and everybody helps take care of Gramma."

John paused. "You must think I'm a goofy old coot, rattling on about myself this way. You're a kind listener, and I know you must be a friend of the Lord because you are a lector and eucharistic minister."

I smiled and thought how easy it is to presume some things by what we see, for none of us is without our dark nights. I said, "I try to be his friend, but I am not always as faithful as I could be. John, I have a few minutes more. Is there anything else you wanted to say?"

"Well, yes, if you don't mind." John went on. "All through our life together we used to tease each other with the old phrase, 'Come grow old with me, the best is yet to be.' Mary has only been ill for two years, so we have known a lot of the best. Even if she doesn't know it, the truly best is not too far for either of us, after we die.

"Mary and I always prayed together. I still kneel by her bed every night and put her rosary with the crucifix in her hand. I don't suppose it means anything to her, but it makes me feel closer to her and closer to the suffering Christ. Sometimes I kneel there for an hour remembering all God's blessings in the seasons of our life. I re-read Ecclesiastes about the times of our life. I don't understand it all, but I suspect this is my time to reap for whatever good we've done and the prayers we've said. I don't have the energy or time to do much of either anymore.

"I do have two prayers of petition: the courage to let her go, and that I don't die before God has taken her. To most folks our life has been ordinary, but like the line in Psalm 17, 'My steps have held fast to your paths; / my feet have not slipped.' We tried to follow him."

I promised to visit him and Mary. He hugged me and said good-bye. I thought, "Ordinary?" His greatness shone through the transparency of his ordinariness. I thought of the words of Mother Teresa: "God has not called us to be successful. He has called us to be faithful." John's is a success story of lived faith.

Prayer Conversations with a Friend

"I was telling the Lord some jokes. Most people tell him their troubles, but once in a while I think he needs a laugh."

In 1979, eleven years before he left us to meet his friend, Cardinal John Dearden spoke of prayer at a Mass for deceased priests: "At death we go to meet the Lord. What a difference there will be between meeting him as close friend to continue a conversation that has been carried on each day for years and years, or meeting him as someone a bit less familiar, someone to whom we are going to have to say some things for the first time."

What does one say to a friend who is God?

At the dinner hour, the shadowy city church was empty except for the old man in the first pew. His suit was green-shiny with wear and age, but a merry look lighted his face. The priest saw him from the sacristy, watched, and wondered. The old man was smiling, nodding, and occasionally slapping his knee as laughter rolled out of him. The next time the priest looked, the old man had made the sign of the cross and was leaving.

The priest met the old man at the church door. "It was nice to hear you laughing."

"Thanks," the old man replied. "I was telling the Lord some jokes. Most people tell him their troubles, but once in a while I think he needs a laugh."

My father experienced that same uncomplicated joy in God's company. In his last years, my father often sat in his leather chair, listening to music and "talking things over" with his unseen friend who sat opposite him. One of my father's favorite musical scores was from *Camelot*. He defined his fondness for it: "As the Lord and I sit here, the lovely images of the title song are like getting a peek at heaven, and we smile at each other. Most of all, I am fond of the song 'If Ever I Should Leave You,' for the Lord reminds me that this is the way he loves us and that he will never leave us, no matter what season."

Missionaries, politicians, social workers, and educators visited my father's room and were exposed to the contagious and practical concern for poor people that I am sure had been the focus of "talking things over" between the two friends.

Poised and cultivated Gerre understands such conversations. Gerre is a caring wife and mother, an accomplished musician, and a dedicated volunteer. We talked recently about prayer. Her face softened, and her voice sped along like quicksilver as she told me why for her the rosary is not the bland, rote prayer some say it is.

Gerre wove a comforting image of how as mothers we never grew bored rocking our babies while singing them lullabies over and over. She added, "Don't you think Mary has the same reaction to our Hail Mary's! It's a love song we're singing to her."

Gerre described an added dimension of her rosary prayer, which she says before Mass each morning. After reflecting on the mysteries of each decade of the rosary, her generous spirit recalls the following: "With the first decade, I pray for family and friends, especially those who are ill; for leaders, scientists, and medical personnel, so they can bring about peace and cures for illnesses. The second, I give thanks for the graces given to my family and for the church, the Eucharist, and forgiveness of sins. After the third, I ask for strength for my family to obey God's will, and mercy for those who are seeking freedom or are alienated. The fourth, I appeal for compassion for those who are without love, for the mentally and physically handicapped, for the insane and criminals, and for those who bring violence. The fifth is a general wrap-up and specifically for those who are to die this day, those who will be gravely tempted, and a request that the Lord will be with me whatever I do."

I have learned the secret that once you have allowed prayer, formal and informal, to become a habit, you cannot break it. You instinctively turn to it whether in the anguish of your life falling apart or in a moment so filled with the exquisite beauty and generosity of God that tears stream down your face in gratitude, and in all the in-between, ordinary times. Unlike the disciples on the road to Emmaus, you are acutely aware that it is Jesus Christ walking beside you. Prayer then becomes a conversation between two friends.

The Spirit Dancing

*Spirit is a word that dances through our thoughts
and conversations.*

"Twenty-five years ago you taught me about 'spirit,'" commented the tall man as he shook my hand and introduced himself at a holiday gathering. "You probably don't remember me, but I've never forgotten you. You were training a group of us drafted parish people to be leaders in the educational program for the Detroit Archdiocesan Synod '69.

"The meeting was instructive and an invitation to be part of a unique adventure. Everyone seemed to catch your spirit of enthusiasm. At the end you did an unexpected thing, at least a surprise to me. You said, 'I sense the Spirit of the Lord moving among us, supporting us, inspiring our efforts. Each of us is essential to the success of Seeking Progress Together, so let's bless each other with an embrace as a sign of our community with each other and the Lord.'

"The group became quiet, awkward as ten-year-olds at a grade school dance. You know, Jane, in 1969, people were not as free with hugs as today. You laughed and said, 'Try it!' and hugged the priest who was part of your team, and then you turned to Archbishop Dearden to embrace him also. He shyly smiled, seemed pleased, but was at a loss for what to do next. He didn't wait long, for the group went on a spree of hugs and handshakes that included him."

Tom went on. "I felt so alive at that moment without being quite sure why. I did acknowledge that it had been a spiritual experience in a very human setting, but was wary, however, of making a big deal of it. It didn't go away like the high after your team wins a big game. I finally saw the light and began the conscious journey to my inner self that directs my life today. I always wanted to thank you and now I will!" With that, he hugged me, and I hugged him back.

I remember that what happened at that gathering in 1969 was as spontaneous for me as it had been for the group. It was a genuine, heartfelt response to a spirit-filled moment that needed to be seized and captured in memory.

Spirit is a word that dances through our thoughts and conversations. I use *dances,* because most of the time its partners are positive, motivating gifts such as the spirit of love, hope, patriotism, sacrifice, courage, loyalty, reverence, and so on.

If we are attentive to the reality of the moment, the positive spirit lifts us out of the humdrum into the exuberant rhythm of the extraordinary. We reach beyond ourselves. We grow. We see differently. We connect with God.

The secret is *being deeply attentive* to your motivation and action. If you are not, you may feel a natural pride in yourself, but you have really missed the boat to deeper growth and spiritual awareness.

An educator, counselor, or friend can affirm the spirit, encourage the person to name it and look inward to its source. In talking it over with another individual, a person often sees more clearly and later, in personal reflection, he or she can identify with his or her deeper self and with others, and find the communion with God that nourishes human spiritual hunger.

We don't need to look very far to find those heroes and heroines who are so busy struggling with the immensity of life that being attentive to the spirit sustaining them or the Spirit of God is nearly impossible. They have a right to call upon *our* spirit of compassion. You may feel unqualified to respond, but try listening to them. Your spirit may surprise you!

"How is Terry?" I asked my friend on the phone.

Her voice lacked its sparkle when she answered. "Not good. The AIDS is progressing, but he's passionately hanging on to life. He's like a tree in a hurricane, bending and springing back. We try not to let him see our pain hiding behind our loving attention. Please pray that we have the guts to go the distance with him.

"This has been a time of such physical and spiritual darkness that the light at the end of the tunnel is barely a flicker. It must be some light beyond us like faith or hope. I don't know anymore. I am so drained I still can't pray. I'm so glad you told me about the words of Mother Teresa: 'When we cannot pray . . . give that inability to [Jesus]. . . . Let Him pray in us to the Father. . . . No one knows the Father better. . . . No one pray[s] better than Jesus.' Those are true words of comfort."

I answered her. "Mary Lou, you and Wally are walking, breathing prayers. Your life has become one continuous prayer. That flicker you see is your own fierce spirit of courage that draws you ever forward. It won't leave you. Neither will the Spirit of the Lord. Terry's life spirit is carrying him until he hands it over in exchange for the new life awaiting him." By then we were both crying, for the nurse had said, "Next month." In the meantime, my friends are on the mysterious road to Calvary. And to the Resurrection.

It is a sad commentary on contemporary life that the world is populated with some persons, guided by positive spirits, who bring good but, for whatever reason, just skim the surface of life and never pause to ponder who they really are or know the indwelling of the God they unconsciously seek.

They are a people who do not see. Are they not calling to those of us who behold the world beyond our five senses to open their eyes?

Love at Work

Loving those we serve is not always easy and often risky,
but we demean ourself and our profession if we do not.

The tiny woman with the short-cropped, graying hair stood alone on the stage with no lectern, no notes, no pretense. The world-renowned Dr. Elisabeth Kübler-Ross chose to be vulnerable with the thousand nurses before her and allowed the passionate fire within her to sear their conscience. She concluded her stories of heroism in the world of healing with, "If you do not love your patients, you must leave the profession!" There it was in a modern meeting hall, the powerful message that Jesus proclaimed.

Deeply moved, the nurses rose to their feet to salute this courageous woman who, like them, had studied hard, experienced all the options, stripped away the trivia, and arrived at the essence: the basic motivation must be love.

Pope John Paul II had given a similar message two years earlier in his 1981 encyclical, "On Human Work," when he said: "Sweat and toil, which work necessarily involves in the present condition of the human race, present the Christian and everyone who is called to follow Christ with the possibility of sharing lovingly in the work that Christ came to do. This work of salvation came about through suffering and death on a cross."

Dr. Kübler-Ross's message, fused with personal beliefs, directed the vocations of the two young nurses who were with me the night of her lecture. My son and daughter have gone on to serve in those areas of nursing where love must be a factor or the job would be impossible.

Jim already had volunteered for assignment in the burn center to which the state's worst cases were flown. Pain relentlessly enveloped the patients there; medical procedures were exacting and exhausting. Asked why he continued, Jim replied: "With the need for extremely sterile conditions, the chaplain often cannot come in, so I talk to the patients about God and bring them messages from their family. It helps them fight for life. I think God wants me to stay here awhile."

For his next assignment, Jim chose the Intensive Care Unit (ICU) connected with the inner-city hospital's emergency room. Constantly shrieking sirens signaled the arrival of those close to death. They were sent directly to ICU, where speed and correct diagnosis pressed hard on the staff. Here, caring for the assembly line of broken bodies was a brutal grind. It easily bred cynicism. Nevertheless, Jim remarked, "You must remind yourself that they are God's creation and treat them respectfully, even if some have not respected themselves. It is gratifying to see their response to our kindness, which in turn helps us give more."

When Therese was assigned to the Intermediate Intensive Care Unit (IICU) in a suburban hospital, the head nurse asked her to see what she could do for Jenny, seventy-nine years old, who had receded into herself with her two companions, bitterness and depression. Jenny had suffered a heart attack after her fifty-eight-year-old son's suicide. Wanting no more of living, she tore away the life-support systems. The hospital personnel tied her hands to the bed, only angering her further.

It took courage for the young nurse to love and be rebuffed. Therese had not known that kind of failure, but she was determined. Therese cared for Jenny, caressed her bruised arms, told her funny stories, and eventually read to her from the Psalms. Slowly, with great delicacy, Therese brought an awakening to the woman.

Jenny recovered rapidly once she saw reasons for living. When she left the IICU, Therese often visited her in the regular room. Weeks later, before she left the hospital to go home, Jenny asked to be wheeled to the IICU to say good-bye to Therese, whom she called "my angel sent by God to bring me back."

Another patient remains vivid in Therese's memory. Eileen, the mother of a nurse friend, was in a life-threatening situation.

Therese said, "I felt that death sat waiting on the other side of the bed. It was like a tug of war." But one evening Eileen seemed stable, and the faithful family left their vigil to eat.

Suddenly the monitor sounded. Eileen opened her eyes and smiled. The monitor indicated that her heartbeat had stopped. Eileen had signed orders that no extraordinary means should be used to resuscitate her.

This was the first time one of Therese's patients had died. Since a chaplain was not available, telling the family became Therese's responsibility. She willed herself to meet them. She stood at the door of the waiting room and whispered the news, but could not stop her own tears. Family and nurse embraced and consoled each other.

Therese had done everything possible but felt "unprofessional" because she cried when informing the family. She confessed her concern to her supervisor. The older, wise supervisor told her: "Grief is an honest emotion for someone you cared about. It is more important that you are as loving as you are. The family spoke to me about your care and compassion, which helped them through their ordeal. You're the kind of nurse we need here."

Loving those we serve is not always easy and often risky, but we demean ourself and our profession if we do not.

The Bible's Power

My spiritual roots have been richly nourished throughout my lifetime, but they still hold, somewhere in their gnarled center, those biblical wonder stories that shaped my identity.

My earliest memories of the Bible are those of my mother reading to me from a thin, tan book of stories for children. For a book intended for young eyes, it was strangely unattractive. The black-and-white drawings had the dour look of Dürer etchings, yet the portrayal of Jesus struggling under the huge cross remains frozen in my memory. It was a mystery to me that no one but Simon of Cyrene helped him. Compassion spurred my courage, and I knew in my child-heart that if I had been there I would have protected him. My spiritual roots have been richly nourished throughout my lifetime, but they still hold, somewhere in their gnarled center, those biblical wonder stories that shaped my identity.

Before Christmas a few years ago, Janemarie, my two-and-a-half-year-old granddaughter, cuddled into my lap and asked, "Read it again, Gramma." She was talking about the story of Mary and Joseph's journey to Bethlehem, their finding no place to sleep except a stable with the animals, the humble shelter where Jesus, the son of God, was born.

Janemarie was familiar with our ritual of placing the figure of the infant in the crib on Christmas Day. On Christmas Eve, she announced to her mother and me, "I'm taking Baby Jesus to bed with me tonight, 'cuz he shouldn't get cold the night before he gets borned." We two women looked at each other, smiled tenderly, and, with a tear or two, were thankful for being in the presence of such loving innocence.

Children who grow up hearing the voice of Jesus speaking to them in the parables possess an extraordinary insight into the meaning of discipleship and are no strangers to the Bible when it is presented at school.

On the other hand, children whose reading diet has been exclusively Mickey Mouse, Superman, or the classic children's stories, must swim against the tide of their own memories when they are finally introduced to the Scriptures. I am not saying that the world of make-believe is wrong. It *is* important to growth, just as exploring the joys of nature expands a child's imagination. Each is good. However, as we try to maintain a balance of food for our child's physical health, we should consciously provide a balance of spiritual stimulation for an impressionable young mind and heart. I have found no better source than the Bible itself told in stories suitable to the age of the child.

An adult who professes to be a Christian but does not know Christ seems somehow unfinished. I met such a man, the son of a casual, older friend. He was badly incapacitated by emphysema. For most of his life he had run after big deals and pretty women. Now in the slow lane, life sat heavily upon him, and the weight of his thoughts was filling in the gap between adolescence and adulthood. Our conversations centered on our mutual interest in the theater. He grew steadily weaker, and I would read parts of plays to him. When I asked if I could read the Scriptures to him, he answered emphatically. "No, I'm no phony!"

He was hospitalized and returned home stronger. When I visited him there, I told him the story of the prodigal son. I reminded him that God was like that father and that God had never stopped loving him. The next visit, he asked, "Is there some easy version of the Bible I could read, maybe one with explanations? Remember, I have a lot of catching up to do."

I returned the following day with a copy of *Share the Word,* a small, paperback magazine published six times a year. It contained the lectionary readings for each Sunday with commentaries and background information, as well as a daily reading guide to the Scriptures. I also laid the New American Bible gently beside him. My friend was delighted when he examined *Share the Word:* "This is great. The explanations are modern and speak to today!"

I see him less frequently now. He remains dependent on "Oscar," his oxygen tank, but his outlook is brighter. He is interested in more things. He chuckled, "It's ironical. I'm still confined, but I no longer feel like I'm on the sidelines watching the parade go by. I don't do much, but I feel more worthwhile. There aren't many visitors, but I don't feel alone. I guess I have a new life. Perhaps this son is returning home."

Bread and Wine

*In Christ's boundless love for us, he brings in his body and blood
a fresh and unique miracle to every person.*

It was a simple meal: a bowl of soup, French bread, and a small
glass of wine. Father Frank Granger had prepared it himself. He
could not afford a cook in his poor inner-city parish. We had been
friends for a long time and been there for each other in sorrow
and joy. The meal followed the Eucharist that we had just celebrated in church in memory of my late husband. There seemed
no break in the holy peacefulness as we moved into Father's
kitchen. Frank is gone now, but no banquet could satisfy me more
physically or fill my spirit with more peace and unity than that
meal of soup, bread, and wine.

The breaking of bread is a communal act. People who, by
force of circumstances, must eat alone often say, "I don't fuss
much anymore. I just eat enough to get by, but I don't enjoy it."

Just as bread is basic to our body, the Eucharist is basic to our
spirit. Jesus assures us, just as he did the crowds who followed
him to Capernaum after he astounded them with the multiplica-
tion of the loaves and fishes: "I am the bread of life. Whoever
comes to me will never be hungry, and whoever believes in me
will never be thirsty" (John 6:35).

In the thirteenth century, Pope Urban defined the Eucharist as
the spiritual food that "fully restores, truly nourishes, completely
satisfies—not the body but the heart, not the flesh but the soul,
not the stomach but the mind."

We twentieth-century people do not deal well with mystery.
Even so, the bread and wine help us to grasp the reality of Jesus'

sacrificing his body and blood for our redemption. We must let ourselves experience God through our senses and our feelings. If we cannot feel, we cannot love. If we cannot love, we have no relationship with Jesus or anyone else.

As a eucharistic minister, I have come to more fully realize both the human and spiritual extraordinariness of the sacrament of the Eucharist. Each person who comes to receive is different, with different needs. In Christ's boundless love for us, he brings in his body and blood a fresh and unique miracle to every person. He satisfies our individual hungers and thirsts.

Should the satisfaction of our hunger not lead us to realize that just as Jesus has been given to us, we as Christ-bearers must give ourselves to others? Is that not what the final words of the priest mean? "Go in peace to love and serve the Lord." Or don't we hear the words in our rush to leave and get on with our life? It is puzzling that we do not always grasp what has happened to us.

Perhaps we can heighten our appreciation of mystery if we look at other cultures and their reverence for bread and its symbolic meanings. A while ago, my daughter Maureen and her family stayed on the Hopi reservation in Arizona. The Hopi, whose name means "Peaceful Ones," celebrate ceremonies throughout the year for the health and prosperity of all living things. Their bread—piki—is made of cornmeal and is part of each ceremony as well as daily ritual. For instance, the sacred cornmeal is sprinkled to mark the outline of a new room to be added to a household.

One Hopi ritual takes place when a woman is about to give birth. She retires to a separate room with her mother and other clan women, taking some sacred cornmeal with her. Twenty days after the child is born, the father, who has not yet seen the child, comes at dawn to sprinkle a path with the sacred cornmeal to the edge of the mesa so that the young Hopi will be properly set on the road of life. The child's mother and the maternal grandmother carry the infant, pray over it, present it to the rising sun, and give the child a name. This essential ritual may be compared to Baptism, with which we initiate our children into the Christian life, or to the sharing of our bread and wine to nourish us.

The Hopi seem greatly sensitive to sacred symbolism. When Maureen purchased Hopi kachina dolls and exquisite pottery, the

Hopi storekeeper sprinkled the purchases with cornmeal and offered a blessing for the art pieces to go on their way. Maureen asked if she could return the blessing. The woman smiled, handed her some cornmeal, and said, "As you leave, sprinkle the cornmeal and pray for the artists."

Realizing our inadequate appreciation of the Eucharist is a step toward discovery. In a rare, grace-filled moment, a revelation may come.

Janemarie, my granddaughter, has a unique sense of who Jesus is. One summer, when she was three-and-a-half, she sat near the front of our small, country church when I was a eucharistic minister. When we returned home, she asked, "Gramma, what were you giving the people?" I replied, "Jesus." She clapped her hands and, with eyes transformed with intensity, cried, "It must be like swallowing sunshine!"

Jesus Comes to an Open Heart

"We are gazing on a mystery of faith: open our heart and Jesus will come in and teach us who he is and who we are."

The hall was empty after the retreat except for a young woman rummaging through her bag. Somehow I knew that she had been stalling for time to see me alone. I followed her lead, pacing her in putting away my notes. She approached me and haltingly asked, "How can I get closer to Jesus?" I replied, "Your presence here today indicates you're already trying."

"Yes," she went on, "but this is an isolated event. If he is the vine, and I'm a branch, I don't feel connected. What can I do to be nourished by him, appreciate him more? Where do I find him? What can I do to change me? In the bad times I turn to him to beg or blame. When things are really super, I sometimes thank him, but most of the time I'm too busy celebrating my good fortune. In reality my life is more often flat and ordinary. My consciousness of his voice is muffled by so many other sounds hassling me."

Beth and I sat at one of the tables, sipping the last of the decaf left in the parish pot and talking about the common human experience—the continual searching for and discovering the reality of God.

I told her the following stories, hoping that they would show her that she was not alone in her discomfort. Others had the same experience, often over and over again. Steve and Millie were such a couple.

They had reached a point in their faith-life that felt like one long winter with no sign of spring in sight. They admitted that listening to the Sunday Scripture readings was like sitting through reruns of old movies, and the sermons didn't help much either. Millie commented that "the sense of God was like a plume of smoke that floated through the service and disappeared before we reached the parking lot."

Then a new assistant priest came to their parish. He told stories that connected the readings to the morning newspaper, movies, community needs, and happenings in the parish. I remember Steve's enthusiasm and the use of his electrical engineering terms when he explained what happened. "Father Dan showed us how to tear away the insulation we had packed around the word of God and let its meaning energize our daily lives! That was five years ago. Millie and I are still continually astonished how each reading calls out to the reality of today. Jesus is very much with us, and we try to make his way ours."

Tony and Becky are another story. At the international airport, they looked like a high-spirited "yuppie" couple setting off for a backpacking vacation in some exotic land. Passersby smiled at them, perhaps with a twinge of envy that their own humdrum lives did not offer such adventure. Adventure it would surely be for Tony and Becky, but different than observers at the airport would have guessed.

Tony and Becky's destination was a small, poor village in Brazil. They would be lay missionary helpers, living with the people and teaching carpentry and basic literacy. Tony, a successful lawyer and amateur handyman, and Becky, a teacher, had been married for eighteen months.

Becky explained their commitment with eloquent simplicity: "As we grew in our love for each other, we became more sensitive to the presence of God in our life together. We needed to say 'thank you,' so this is the way we are doing it: by serving the poor and, through them, learning the meaning of really loving God as he loves us."

And Herb found yet another way. Jovial and fifty-five, he was laughing at himself when he related his experience at a parish Rite of Christian Initiation of Adults (RCIA) meeting. "When I was asked to be a sponsor for a prospective member of the church, I wasn't sure what I was walking into. I thought I was going to be the 'giver.' I was wrong. I didn't have all the answers. Doug, my candidate, and I grew together as we studied with the catechist and each other. My eyes were opened to how much I could learn about the faith I had lived all my years!

"Secondly, I thought the whole process would be on a friendly, helpful, but somewhat impersonal basis. Wrong again. Doug was received into the church two years ago, and he became like a brother, as well as a dear friend. His love of the Lord shines forth from him, and I am humbled and grateful to come to Jesus through him. I really didn't know where I was walking when I accepted the role of sponsor, but I now think it was the road to Emmaus."

Discovering and rediscovering Jesus can happen in a magical instant, but it usually is a slower process. In fact, we trust the more measured pace because by nature we are not prepared for the unexpected from the Divine.

At the end of our conversation in the parish hall, Beth concluded, "We are gazing on a mystery of faith: open our heart and Jesus will come in and teach us who he is and who we are."

Easter People

*"I want to be a person giving God my best
rather than the straggly edges."*

"If belief in Jesus doesn't make me different, why bother? Why go
through the motions? I don't know. A lot of questions are spooking
around in my head. I don't see my faith dealing with my reality. My
friend Liz overdosed last month. That was real. Strange, liberated
Liz said she was a river exploring the land. Did she know she was
on the edge of a precipice? People say Liz and I are alike, but my
river is aimless, meandering out of habit and still teasing me with
the disguise of freedom. Freedom for what? Maybe freedom means
charting a course and freely following it. I don't know."

These were Tess's troubled, lonely thoughts four years ago.
This year the smiling, freckled, lean young woman in the no-name
jeans and I met again at a seminar on gerontology. We discussed
our reasons for attending, especially her intense interest in helping the people she calls "hers."

Tess continued her earlier story. "Liz's death made me look at
life. My process was no joy ride. I began to wonder if I was one
of the walking dead that Mother Teresa spoke about in a lecture I
heard. Life was gray fog. Where was my spirit? Where was *the*
Spirit of the Lord?

"I read a small notice on the campus activities board asking
for summer volunteers to work in Appalachia. Why not, I thought.
At least I might move myself out of this stagnant pool I'm floun-
dering in. My hope was that in helping someone else, the Lord
might make himself known to me. He did say, 'Seek and you will
find,' didn't he?

"It happened. He was there with the women weeding the vegetable patch. He was down at the coal mines, where crevices of black dust line the men's faces. He was there in the edges of the small schoolroom where the children and I taught each other games to learn numbers. He was heard in the music, sweet and sad, from the fiddler's bow, and he hovered around the old folks, even helped me tuck the big napkin under Grandpop's chin."

Tess smiled and went on. "The mystery of mysteries became clearer. That pallid, passive, fragile thing I called faith was transformed into an exuberant, passionate, straightforward relationship with the Divine, that Being I thought could not touch me. In a way, Liz brought me out of my tomb to new life. I guess I am an Easter person!"

Dan is another Easter person. He had a dream, heard a sermon, and changed his life. No mystical visions, no miracles, just plain everyday happenings infused with Dan's openness to the grace of the moment. Dan told me of the dream. "I was on a subway in the back of a train that was careening dizzily from left to right. One minute the unfriendly crowded pushing me had strange inhuman faces, and the next they were all people I knew. They were crowding and squeezing, too. The lights went out. The car seemed out of control, going faster and faster. I awoke in a terrified sweat. I lay there, asking myself, 'What did I do to bring that on?'"

Dan continued. "The next morning, the Sunday before Ash Wednesday, at Mass the visiting priest spoke about looking at Lent through new lenses. 'Some folks need to look at their lives with microscopes for things they never see that need changing; some should look through binoculars for visions of what they could become for God. Then make your judgment about what you will do for Lent.'

"When the family and I returned home, I said I had to run over to the store. I felt I could explain this small deception once I understood it myself. Out of the car, the freezing vapors stung my face and cleared out all but the issues of the moment. I visited a small art gallery. While I sat at a corner table with a mug of hot coffee, the dream and the sermon tumbled with meanings.

"I began to sort things out and heap them up in the corners of my mind. The tallest pile was labeled 'time.' Time had become my relentless master. I was programmed every day, moving from one deadline to another, pushing in periods with my family or for brief relaxation. There was no space to spare for prayer.

"Then I remembered the priest's story of the microscope. I saw that time is neutral but that I had allowed it to be the master. Why? Money? I guess so. It was that second computer job in the evenings that shredded my control over my life. We were doing okay with Martha's and my incomes, but when the chance came for more money and the extras it could buy, we didn't anticipate the consequences of what it took from us as a family and from me as a person.

"I would like to learn to live in a way in which my senses are awake, when I'm not too tired and have the freedom to walk on the shores, hike in the woods, ride the Ferris wheel! I want time for thinking about curiosities, beauty, and the mysteries of life. But most of all, I want to be a person of real faith commitment, available when someone, especially my family, needs me. I want to be a person giving God my best rather than the straggly edges."

The stories of Tess and Dan show the possibilities of transformation when faith is really lived. They are Easter people.

Imagination:
Setting Us Free, Warming Our Soul

*"When you are scared and miserable, logic is of little comfort.
Imagination warms the soul."*

One day in late September, my daughter, Therese, and her daughters, Janemarie (four) and Emily (ten months), and I visited the Detroit Zoo. We followed the elephant tracks painted on the cement path. Somehow, in our absorption with the animals, we wandered onto a side path. Janemarie noticed the difference. "We lost the elephant tracks!" she exclaimed. "But are we lost?" I asked. With the patience of a child trying to instruct an adult, she replied, "No, Gramma, you have a zoo map. It will tell us how to get back."

We walked on, and Therese quietly said: "This reminds me of one of my favorite images of God—the story of a person who had a dream of looking back over a lifetime of walking with the Lord. They were on a long beach, and there were two sets of footprints in the sand. However, at times there was only one set, and those were at the person's periods of sadness and difficulty. The person questioned, 'Lord, you said that once I decided to follow you, you would walk with me. But when I needed you most, you left my side.' The Lord answered, 'My child, I never left you during your times of trial. Where you see only one set of footprints, I was carrying you.'"

Therese, a nurse, continued. "This image sustains me especially when I am on duty on the twelve-hour night shift. In the intensive care unit, there is little time for breaks. Sometimes I grow very weary, and I whisper, 'Help me, Lord.' I feel lighter, like strong, tender arms have lifted me. You don't need to be dead like Lazarus to have new life breathed into you.

"Sometimes my patients will express fear that God has forgotten them or that the illness is a punishment from him. I tell them the story of the footprints in the sand and of the continuous love of God. Then we may speak of God's faithfulness to persons in the Bible, or the patients tell me stories of faithfulness in their own lives. The storytelling seems to release good memories of the past and hope for the future. Like the zoo map, it leads the people back to faith and trust in the image of a faithful God."

"Your patients are fortunate that you can tap into their imagination through the footprints story," I told her. "A great many adults do not allow their imagination to lead them to new patterns of thinking of God and moral awareness. Many modern theologians believe that adults may grow in faith more through developing fresh images than through logic or reason."

Therese smiled and replied, "When you are scared and miserable, logic is of little comfort. Imagination warms the soul. It is truly a gift from God."

We continued to push the stroller and listen to Janemarie's creative descriptions. "A zebra is really a horse that God disguised for Halloween and liked it so much that ever since, the zebra was born with stripes."

I told Therese of an experience I had during the summer. "The mother of one of my Bible School students asked me, 'Help me become as excited about my faith as my son is about the parables you have been discussing this week.'

"In our conversation I soon discovered she wasn't excited about herself or anything else. Here was a woman time had passed by. Women's independence was alien to her. She was still looking for her identity in a man. Her man had left her. Hopelessness was now her guiding delusion.

"When she came back after class the next day, I told her: 'In seeking creative insights to difficult problems, we need to dialog with ourself—state our ideas and listen to them. We evaluate by imagining alternative actions, looking at the positive and negative. If we run into a dead end, we begin dialoging with a new idea. A little later we seek the ideas of others in face-to-face dialog or through books and articles. Right now, I would like you to read this book, *Fried Green Tomatoes at the Whistle Stop Cafe*, and have a conversation with two of the central characters, Evelyn Couch and Mrs. Threadgoode. Then come see me, and we will talk about what image or images you have of yourself. While you are reading, link the story of God in the Scriptures to the story of your own experience, blending childhood memory, family stories, reflection, and the inspiration you get from the book. Use of your imagination can teach you how to find meaning and burst through the bounds of old images, preconceptions, and unaskable questions.'

"I also told her that strong imagination imagines the truth; it does not wander about seeking wild or trivial fantasies. We must constantly figure out what is authentic, what squares with God-truth, and make it part of our life. Imagination sets us free to mature, to become more fully human, to find meaning and values out of past experiences that we may have regretted or even carried around in a yoke of guilt.

"She waited three weeks before she visited me. A different woman stood at my door: stylish outfit, new hairstyle, and she was smiling. She hugged me, and the words came tumbling out: 'I read the book many times. My conversation with Evelyn became more intimate—about meeting the expectations of my parents to be a nice young lady and of a husband who never let me finish a sentence. Mrs. Threadgoode kept reassuring me that I was an important somebody. For the first time I really began to talk to God, not just recite prayers.

"'I couldn't come back sooner, Jane, because I was so darned mad. I had allowed myself to be submerged in a hopeless rut of thinking the same thing over and over again: nobody will love you, you're not nice enough, you're not docile enough. My image of myself was a rug that everyone walked all over but didn't care about.

"'Thank you for helping me look at myself, my life, my history. I foolishly thought I had myself somewhat together, but I discovered I was hanging wide open. I have a long way to go to change my image, but like Evelyn, I'll make it. And incidentally, faith *is* more exciting now that I dialog with God!'"

The Wisdom of Children

*Parenting was sunshine and shadow. In the arena
of the gray areas, the pros and cons were played out
when mind and heart dueled.*

When we are open, we grow through every relational encounter.
If we learn more from our children, perhaps it is because we see
ourselves in them. Or, perhaps much is learned because in loving
our children so greatly, we can also be hurt more deeply. I think it
is both.

Enlightenment does not occur in a vacuum. Truthful compre-
hension cannot happen unless illusions are stripped away about
the family situation, whether it be supportive or destructive, happy or anguished, open or closed. Ideally, the Christian family will
learn from each other in a climate diffused with a consciousness
of the presence of God in each person. The common ground is
caring for and about each other.

Hopefully my learning experiences as a parent-pupil will
shed some light for other parents in similar circumstances.

While each child may have a different timetable, the inevitabil-
ity of a parent's letting go awaits like a celebratory sacrament. Since
childhood, our son Michael was an inward explorer. Fueled by a
persistent curiosity and inventive imagination, he excelled in knowing how things worked and won awards in school science fairs. He
was a planner, a builder, prizing his home, his workshop, and his
family.

However, the restless culture of the 1960s slashed at his roots.
At seventeen, he wanted to be free to explore outer worlds by

wandering across the country. His father's foot came down with an emphatic "No!"

I reminded my husband, Gene, that other of our children had gone away to school or college. He challenged, "They were in supervised environments, while Michael would be thrown into a brutal world of harsh survival."

"It scares me too," I agreed, "but he may go with or without our permission. Can't you remember what it was like when you were seventeen?"

Gene and I had learned that parenting was sunshine and shadow. In the arena of the gray areas, the pros and cons were played out when mind and heart dueled.

This time, the mind said: "If Michael stays home out of forced obedience, he could resent our decision the rest of his life for the promise he could not keep with his destiny. If he leaves in defiance, with our mutual hurt and anger seeping into his soul, he may exchange his normal caution for a cocky, 'I'll show them!'"

At the same time, the heart was murmuring: "This young man is our son, whom we have guided. He is strong and resourceful. He does not dance to a whimsical tune. Send him forth with our prayerful blessing, trusting in his basic goodness and good sense. He believes he is ready. He needs our love and trust. We must let go in generosity and not because we are afraid not to."

With words of advice for the road and kisses salty from tears, we wished Michael, "Godspeed, son, you go with our love and the hope that this will be a great adventure. We will always be here for you."

The process had been pressured. We did not have years to decide, although in reality we had been leading up to this time all his life. It was a painful education, revealing our overprotective, mythic fears and our delusions of always knowing what is best for our children because we are the parents, and also reliving the bittersweet memories of our own individual struggles to gain adult independence.

Somehow, at the time, the time never seems right for letting go. And sometimes it isn't. Parents must be absolutely honest, especially about who they are protecting: the child or themselves. Once the decision is made, there is an emotional and spiritual satisfaction that you have been mature enough to trust God, your child, and yourselves. A new relationship is formed. You become friend as well as parent.

In 1972 when Jack and I were married, bringing together fifteen children with two family histories and traditions, we had ambitious hopes of building a happy, unified life together and of healing the still-open wounds from the deaths of the Hugheses' mother and the Wolfords' father. In the beginning, the hoped-for life was as elusive as the dream that floats away once you awaken.

Learning from newly acquired stepchildren was different than learning from a child with whom you had sat through a feverish night or cheered for a touchdown that won the game or grieved a young love who wandered off. Jack was learning also, but this is my story.

I had no common memories, no personality road maps to guide me. The Hughes children were hungry for what once was, and I had not been part of it.

I tried to understand. I was alive; their mother wasn't. I had their father's love. They were afraid he would love them less. I was the stranger. Wanting to learn, I steeled myself to cope with subtle forms of distrust, fear, rejection. I was not always successful.

In bending to keep peace, I pushed my normal reactions into an uncomfortable straight jacket. I felt like a gambler playing for high stakes.

I had come wanting to love and be loved. I also knew that love and trust could not be forced, but I wasn't even enforcing the simple rules we had mutually set. Jack and I looked upon the communal evening meal as essential to our bonding: preparing the food, praying, eating, and sharing together. No one living at home was excused without very good reason. One evening, as we assembled around the table, Paul, age six, exploded. "I'm not going to eat now. My brothers and sisters said you aren't my mother, so I don't have to obey you!"

His big eyes were brimming with tears as I pulled him to me in the silence weighted with words unspoken. I softly said, "Paul, I know I'm not your mother, but let's talk about this. Mrs. B. is your substitute teacher while Sister is sick. You obey her, don't you?" A low "yes" was whispered. I went on. "I'm like a substitute mother. I hope someday you and your brothers and sisters will learn to love me not as your mother, who cannot be replaced, but maybe as a friend who loves you. In the meantime, I expect you and everyone else to follow the rules of our home so we can have some happiness together as a family."

From then on I was able to be me. I learned that my personal integrity was not a gambler's coin to risk. I had never done it before, nor have I since.

Shared life sandpapered the roughness of our differences and gradually the tensions became the ordinary tensions between people who try to love one another. The last twenty-two years have been a busy blend of graduations, weddings, births, divorces, hospitals, gravesides, and all the small groupings that make the many large gatherings possible and fun. We lean toward each other like the giant redwoods, reaching for our common sunshine of caring about each other.

What have I been learning? To be there, be there. Be there if not in person, then in spirit. It's not new. Jesus said it two thousand years ago.

Christ's Place, the Workplace

Catholics are part of the solutions or part of the problems in the workplace.

The fires that engulfed the Las Vegas high-rise hotel blew cinders of fear that ignited panic in rescue units across the country. How could people trapped in the upper stories be saved?

My son John, who worked in an Emergency Medical Service (EMS) unit in the inner city of Detroit, volunteered for training that would involve scaling tall buildings and being lowered by helicopter to reach choking, frightened prisoners in their rooms. I mentally agreed that training was essential, but I prayed, "God, why my son?"

While on the job, John had been held hostage, shot at, and thrown from the emergency van as it careened around a corner on its mission of mercy. He faced a demanding, unending chaos of brokenness. Most of the patients were victims of human or mechanical violence. Mangled and torn, they appeared almost inhuman. Even though the EMS staff worked frantically, death, the opposing team, often won.

Nevertheless, John remained cheerfully committed to keeping his concern for personal danger at bay while he responded to the disaster calls of those in trouble. Before he left for the high-rise training he must have sensed my reluctance, so he explained his thinking. "Mom, the modern good Samaritan must overcome today's obstacles and barriers that prevent saving and caring. I *have* to go. It's what God wants me to do." So off he went, with my blessing, on his road to Jericho.

His insight is valuable and significant. Each of us is an instrument of the creative power of God, who has called us through our gifts and our work to make the world a better place.

In the service of God, all constructive work is important no matter how menial it may seem to us. In the *Pastoral Constitution on the Church in the Modern World,* Vatican Council II asked us "to discharge [our] earthly duties conscientiously." Prayer will help us remember that we are not alone in our work. As Teilhard de Chardin said, God "is at the tip of my pen, my spade, my brush, my needle—of my heart and of my thought."

If we have felt like a nobody, doing an unappreciated, boring job, we can see ourself and what we do in a different light. We are working with a divine partner, and we *are* important, especially if we contribute the values of our faith to our workplace.

While in his early thirties, my youngest son, Joseph, became a member of the board of directors of a prestigious organization. My husband, Jack, and I visited his workplace for an open house. We were delighted when the president took us aside to tell us: "We're proud to have Joseph as part of our management team. His open-door policy and respectful relationship with the employees has the rest of us reviewing our own work style. He's made a difference around here."

Later, we saw an illustration of what the president had referred to. We were in line for the buffet table when a man came up to Joseph and said, "I have a little problem I would like to discuss with you when you have the time." With a welcoming smile, Joseph answered, "I'm pretty well filled for tomorrow, Steve, but I'll come in early if you can." Steve looked pleased, but a trifle embarrassed. "I don't want to put you out but, sure, I can be in early. You name it." Joseph's answer was apparently typical of the way he worked. "It's no problem. It's what we're here for, Steve, to help each other. See you at seven thirty."

Sue, a hairdresser, has also looked at the reality of her situation. She listens all day to women pouring out their life stories. Sue could soothe them in agreement, but she gently zeros in on their conscience and helps them look at their lives: the care of an elderly relative who is resented, the violation of human respect in cheating on a husband, the dangers of giving in to a child's whims rather than helping him or her grow in responsibility. She does not give answers but tries to release the goodness and good sense that is there.

We don't have to be the boss to help change the office from a gossiping, suspicious, gloom-and-doom atmosphere to one permeated with cooperation and caring. Our actions can be contagious. As we continue, we will gain strength because we will be living in tune with our own integrity and the ultimate meaning of our existence. Inevitably, in some instances, our efforts will cost us. We will be taking on the cross of Christ.

The examples of John, Joseph, and Sue are hopeful, but what about those persons who seem to cut their ties (if any) with weekend religion and sail off by their own compasses all week? Some are little different than the pirates of old. They plunder through "deals," overcharging, manipulating, lying, cheating, and stealing. Like the old pirates, the ends are similar: money and power. The bottom line is to not be caught or to be able to heap the guilt on someone else.

Over one quarter of American adults are Catholics. We cannot point our collective finger at those other guys as the evil moguls. Illegal transactions in the millions of dollars are wrong, but so are laziness, sloppy standards, and unjust practices in the workplace. Catholics make corporate decisions, do scientific research, practice and make laws, work on assembly lines, push brooms, and are unemployed. We are a cross section of America. Catholics are part of the solutions or part of the problems in the workplace.

If we really believe in our faith, we must bring its teachings with us to everything we do. We cocreate with God. We should be making a difference!

Balancing

"I was so depressed I thought I would jump out of a high window like the big shots do, but every week your smile and kindness told me things are not as bad as I thought."

I arrived at Judy's gift shop just as a woman bolted out the door, bumped into me, and continued running to the parking lot, as intent as a finalist in a marathon.

When I entered, Judy was at the cash register shaking her head. "Can you imagine a grown woman getting hysterical over not being able to buy a box of lavender candles! She's running now to another store, and it's almost closing time. She's not the only one. If the store is out of something, people take it as a personal insult. What's happening? Some people seem to have lost their sense of proportion. Every frustration sets off the fireworks of Mount Saint Helens. Do you think those meditation tapes and breathing exercises really relieve stress?"

"I guess they work," I replied. "I know people who use them, but in some cases it's like applying a Band-Aid when surgery is needed. We are all subject to worries, and how we handle them has a lot to do with our view of life, ourself, and others."

Her mention of the candles reminded me of an incident that happened on my twelfth birthday, when we had invited a small group of my friends for cake and ice cream. So I told Judy about it.

The Great Depression had leveled our life to essentials, but my mother believed that celebrations were necessary to paint what could have been a drab life with the sunshine of mystery, gaiety, and beauty. Just before the party was to begin, we discovered that our cache of birthday candles did not have twelve that matched.

Undaunted, my mother decorated the cake like Jacob's coat. When she lighted the colored candles, she did so with the flair of a ringmaster announcing the main act. She told my friends: "As you grow, every year is different and each one special. I hope you won't forget that."

My mother had her priorities in order. She met trying situations head-on and cut them down to size, invented alternatives, or philosophically accepted the unchangeable. She lived through sad and trying times. People would say, "Your mother is so strong." I knew she was as vulnerable as anyone else, but she had the ability to stand back and look at the world with clear and loving eyes. Her strength lay in relying on God and her security in knowing who she was. Being her own person, she was an independent thinker for her time. This story made me think of another one, so I told it to Judy too.

One hot, summer afternoon my mother and I were taking down the wash in the backyard. We could hear the rattle of the approaching battered wagon and the clomp-clomp of the old horse with the caved-in back. The driver's voice was weak as he harshly called out, "Any rags, paper, or bottles today?" My mother went to the fence and asked him if he would like a drink of water and some for his horse. He was grateful.

The men who scoured the alleys in the 1930s were called alley-men, and they dwelled on the lowest rung of the social ladder. This man also wore the broad-brimmed black hat of the immigrant Jew. The simple kindness that my mother showed to Vinnie brought the scrutiny of meddlesome neighbors who came whispering unpleasant predictions of dangers destined to befall us. As each person left our house, swaggering in their self-righteousness, my mother would whistle a lively tune and grin. I discovered it was her secret way of calling forth her good sense and courage.

Vinnie stopped regularly. We learned of the oppression his family had suffered in Russia, of his modest shop in New York, and of the harsh days in the alleys of Detroit. One day he came to our back door with an almost-new trash can on his shoulder. He said, "Missus, I found this in the alley behind one of those big houses where the people had been evicted. The one you have is rusting out, so I'll take yours and leave this one."

My mother said, "Thank you, Vinnie, but I can't pay you." He replied, "You have given me more than money. You saved my life. I was so depressed I thought I would jump out of a high window like the big shots do, but every week your smile and kindness told me things are not as bad as I thought."

Judy agreed that we must know what is important to us, know ourself, and see through society's hypocrisies and contradictions.

Art was another person who understood how to keep balance. Art is a second-generation owner-manager of a quality restaurant, who juggles endless details, unexpected problems, and prima donna personalities. Asked how he achieves this, he answered, "I grew up in this business. I have seen persons who thought they *were* the restaurant and let it consume them. They glowed brightly at first, but in the end they burned out. I love this place, but I have learned to delegate so I don't become absorbed. I've also learned to listen to my body. If I feel good, I can deal with almost any crisis. I get plenty of sleep, work out at the gym three days a week, eat a healthy diet, relax with my family, and look at videos of old-time comedies. My wife is very supportive and understanding, which makes my lifestyle possible."

Art learned early. Others take more time before they even look at their stress-filled lives.

Jay and Ann were close to walking away from one another. In some ways they had already left. Both were in their early thirties, ambitious, high achievers whose days were tightly stacked with layers of individual activities. When they were together, they were often preoccupied, tense, and sometimes critical of what the other did or did not do in maintaining their small, elegant condo.

Ann told me that one evening last summer Jay confronted her: "I asked you to get a six-pack today. It's your turn to shop. We don't have anything cold to drink!" Ann had excused herself, "Sorry, I didn't have time, I'll go now." Jay retaliated. "You never have time for anything, not even me! I'm going to a bar where I can get what I want!"

Ann confessed how shaken she was. She wandered from room to room, holding herself tightly as if to comfort herself. She didn't know what to do. Then in an inspired moment she brought back the memory of her grandmother, who had survived the loss of her husband and two sons in the coal mines of Pennsylvania. "I remembered my grandmother telling me, 'When life becomes too much, talk to God, and put your hands to work: bake, clean, dig in the garden. Don't sit and mope. Do something. It will clear your mind, granddaughter!'"

She went on. "I looked in the refrigerator. I said, 'Whose turn is it to clean? Oh, what does it matter!' The salad bin was soggy with wilted lettuce and scallions. The cheese truly had moldy chunks of some undefined masses. I decided to take everything out, wash, and discard. My mind was busy, but somehow I was calm. I realized the fridge had been neglected just like my marriage. It's true I had not had time for anything. My job and getting my MBA had scheduled my time and energy. I wondered if it was all worth it.

"I was emptying the trash bag of discards when Jay came in. He seemed different. He said, 'I didn't go to a bar. I walked in the park and watched dads pushing their kids on the swings and thought about us. Are you satisfied with our life, or perhaps I should say lives? I'm not, and I'd like to talk.'"

Ann told how they talked into the night. They called into their respective offices the next day to take rarely used personal time off. They examined the cause of their strain. Ann said, "We both could see we were trying to do too much in too little time."

Jay volunteered to give up some of the organizations he had used as contacts for his brokerage firm. Ann decided to take fewer classes, pushing her MBA farther into the future. "We have begun to live by a calendar rather than a ticking clock. Our life is so much more relaxed. We have time for each other. It's wonderful. And Jay is looking forward to joining the dads at the park with the child we're expecting!"

There are many individual answers to maintaining balance. They seem to converge on a recognition of our dependence on God, a clear idea of who we are and what we value in life, what we expect from others, a sense of humor, and the humbling, basic concept that the world was not designed as our personal playpen.

Lifted Up in Sacrifice

Her commitment was so powerful and her sacrifice so complete and unselfish that her life became a sacrament of love and grace.

On Tom's fortieth birthday, his bowling team surprised him with a party. Usually a moderate drinker, Tom was exhilarated by the show of camaraderie and not conscious of the amount of alcohol he had imbibed. On his trip home, he drove off the road. He was ticketed and told to appear in court.

The judge lectured Tom about drinking and driving, but because of his good record, Tom did not lose his license. He was sentenced to spend one hundred hours in community service over the next six months. He was given the name of his parole officer and a list of agencies he might serve.

His stupid disregard of his own and other people's safety embarrassed Tom, and thoughts of what might have happened made him sick. He knew that he had to redeem himself in his own eyes as well as in the eyes of God, his family—especially his children— and his friends.

He prayed for guidance. The words of Saint Paul kept re-echoing in his mind: "Do not be conformed to this world, but be transformed by the renewing of your minds, so that you may discern what is the will of God—what is good and acceptable and perfect" (Romans 12:2). Tom decided that he would choose the service that would hold the greatest possibility for transformation and would be the most difficult penance for him.

Thus, filled with nameless dread, he arrived at the door of the nursing home for the elderly poor.

Sister Marie of the Little Sisters of the Poor greeted him, but since she was pathetically understaffed, she had no time for orientation. She briskly outlined Tom's duties: take the wheelchair patients to the dining room, help feed those who are unable to feed themselves, and take them back to their rooms. With a map and the patients' names and room numbers in hand, he was on his own to begin his reparation.

That night, Tom reported to his wife, Kim. "The facility was clean, but I caught my breath at the odors of illness, age, and poverty. I wondered if they would penetrate my clothes like the smell of smoke. Then I said to myself, 'Don't be petty, this penance isn't supposed to be a picnic, so get on with it.'"

He continued. "My first patient, Steve, was strapped to his wheelchair. He had a partly finished solitaire game on a plywood square on his lap. I introduced myself and, Kim, a weird thing happened. I knew why God had called me to do this penance. When Steve looked up at me with eyes like cloudy blue marbles, the fear that lurked in my heart lunged out at me. I saw myself! Someday this could be me!"

In his one hundred hours, Tom heard many stories of broken lives and surrendered hopes that filled him with sympathy, but never again did he enter the home in dread. He had named his fear, and God had washed it away. Tom continued to serve, to play rummy with Steve, and to bring fresh flowers to "his ladies." Kim and the three children often joined Tom in helping Sister Marie. They did not look upon it as a penance but as acts of atonement for the sins of a society that had broken the poor souls at the home.

The second story of a penitential person in our times is of Rose, a woman whose whole life had been a sacrifice of self for her people, poor African Americans, whom she felt were "not different. They had the right to belong, and a good education would be their bridge."

In the mid-1920s, Rose became one of the first black teachers in the city. She was outstanding. Her master's degree in literature allowed her to weave the magic of stories in her classes, but her greatest talent was to instill confidence, self-esteem, and strong values in her students. A listing of her former students reads like a Who's Who of successful African Americans.

A prominent black lawyer told me: "When you were in Miss Rose's class you worked very hard. She would not tolerate laziness or whining, but if you tried, she gave you everything she could. During the Great Depression, she brought us food and clothes that she got from charitable agencies. Coming from Miss Rose, it didn't feel like you were taking handouts. We were family."

I first met Miss Rose after she had retired and we were both working in literacy programs. I felt her outrage at the desperate situation of the adults before us. She declared: "They were defeated before they started. It is so unjust!" Her commitment was so powerful and her sacrifice so complete and unselfish that her life became a sacrament of love and grace.

I once asked her why she had given up so much. "You didn't marry. You refused advancements, although I understand you had many offers to do supervisory work. You live modestly and still plunge into serving others even though you are nearly blind."

"Don't worry about me. I'll get my advancement when the time comes," Rose replied. "I was no heroine. Those children needed me. I was proud to be a part of their lives." Then she looked at me shyly and smiled. "You know as well as I do what the Lord said, 'If anyone wishes to be my disciple, she must deny herself, take up her cross, and follow me.'"

Rose didn't wait too long after that for her "advancement." And when she was gone we began to realize how much she had given and given, and the meagerness of our own efforts. It helped us understand how much we all need the generous sacrifice of others to lift us up or just get by.

Forming a Family

*When you see your children molding the soft clay of their own
children's personalities with the values you have passed on,
you get a peek at immortality.*

If fostering unity is a desirable way of strengthening family life under ordinary circumstances, it becomes a practical necessity in a
second marriage involving large numbers of children. In either situation, the mystery of family unity has the same vague eccentrici-
ties as the mystery of human relationships. We know a good
relationship without being able to define it in the same way we
know we are in the presence of a strong family.

On 1 June 1972, my husband, Jack, and I humbly and bravely
made a covenant to bring our two groups of children together,
creating a new family. The eight girls and seven boys, ages six to
twenty-eight, had been grieving the loss of a beloved parent for
three years. They were hurting, wary, even suspicious, but they
trusted us enough to hope with us.

The first inspired thing we did was to include all of them as
our attendants in giving us away at the wedding. Dressed in new
formal attire, these young people sensed their individual impor-
tance and agreement in the ritual of handing over their mother or
father to the others.

Thus began our legacy of not choosing favorites among the
children or pitting one against the other in comparisons or competition. This did not mean that every child was treated the same
all the time. We have walked a tightrope in trying to respect their
individual needs, nurture their unique talents, and give space to
their diverse personalities. There have been times when one or

another person has received more attention, more financial help, or more emotional support. As situations shifted, different persons became centers of focus and, as we matured and grew as a family, brothers and sisters joined in the circle of care.

Many times, however, confidentiality was vigorously protected out of respect for the person or the delicacy of the circumstances. Early on, young tattlers and older gossips gained nothing but frowns and often censure. This attitude has been passed on to the grandchildren. As Elena, age seven, says, "If you can't say anything nice, don't say anything at all."

Perhaps our greatest strength has come through trying to make the family a fixed point in a confusing, moving world. To be there for each other is expected of everyone, although it is rarely verbalized. An instinctive, primordial longing to belong and protect the clan seems to motivate each member of the family, which now includes twenty-five grandchildren.

Being there has meant watching two infants fight for their life and seeing them today, whole and embracing life. It has meant the adventure of being "second coach," cheering on a daughter to give birth to a namesake. It has meant listening to the unburdening of heavy hearts, facing the shattering effects of the five divorces we experienced, and sharing in their eventual healing in happy marriages.

Most of the time it has meant celebrations: little Elaine's pure, clear voice soaring through the church at the children's Mass, Joey's speeding the puck past the goalie, and Amie's dancing her heart out in the high school musical. Family gatherings are commonplace, and Christmas is a sacred tradition.

We have tried to live by two strong principles: unconditional love and trust. Unconditional love has often meant accepting when we don't agree and giving a welcoming hug to those who have left. Trust in God and ourself has meant hoping that we have done the best we could, admitting we were wrong when we were, and letting go at the right time.

Has uniting our family been worth it? You bet! Everything pales in comparison to the noisy house filled with laughter and family jokes and stories told and retold. When you see your children molding the soft clay of their own children's personalities with the values you have passed on, you get a peek at immortality.

This year we received a valentine from our son Michael and his wife, Joanne. It may help demythologize what we did. "There are only two lasting bequests you can hope to give your children. One of these is roots, the other wings. Thank you for giving us both."

My Lamborghini Is Only a Poster

Economic justice and living simply are a matter of proportion.

My grandson, who was then seven but who knew more about cars than most adults, presented me with a poster of a red, sleek, exciting Lamborghini Countach. He announced: "Gramma, I know you would love to have this car, so I got this poster for you. I know you wouldn't buy it." Curious, I asked, "Why do you think I wouldn't?" (The question was unnecessary rhetoric, for the whole idea was out of proportion with our standard of living. Yet, I must admit, the twenty-three-year-young woman within me was already pressing her toe to the accelerator!) Christopher replied, "It's very expensive, and you use your money to help poor people have food and clothes."

Who needs a Lamborghini when your heart can be sent racing with the knowledge that you have conveyed to at least one person the wisdom that personal action requires something beyond the swamp of self-satisfaction!

There are some people who feel that the message of the U.S. Bishops' pastoral on *Economic Justice for All* was a fruitless battering of lofty principle against the strongly held American dream of "making it big and living it up!" Those people are right if we forget who we are. They are wrong if we agree with the words of the pastoral: "We know that, at times, in order to remain truly a community of Jesus' disciples, we will have to say 'no' to certain aspects in our culture, to certain trends and ways of acting that are opposed to a life of faith, love, and justice."

The pastoral does not presume, as some believe, to give all the answers to our economic imbalance, but it hopes to create an openness to dialog, to get us in touch with the reality of where we stand as persons and as a community, and to draw us to conversion. The parish community cannot bully or push the people into transformation, even when there is a need for it. It can provide models and opportunities for open and honest dialog.

In the dialog, we should be conscious of the red herrings that distract attention from the much broader and deeper moral and social questions. What exact role should we attribute to money in human life? To what extent are we willing to subordinate the acquisition of the best that money can buy to other social and moral values such as economic justice? Or, to put it in another, simpler way: What significance does money play in my interpretation of personal happiness?

Without, and even with, the communal dialog, what can the average family do to avoid following the culture's script about material needs? With courage and discipline, families must seek ways to simplify their lifestyle, to meet desires with prayer and reflection, and to remember the poor.

Remembering the poor is not possible without knowing some poor persons. We can more easily dismiss "the poor" if we have never seen their eyes, felt their hopelessness, exchanged their dirty clothes for fresh ones, eaten with them, laughed and cried with them, and seen ourselves in them. "There but for the grace of God, go I."

The parish that cares about poor people often adopts another less economically fortunate parish and can connect the two groups of God's people. Uncomfortable as it may be at times, we cannot easily eliminate hurting human beings out of our heart and consciousness once we have met them. Saying "no" to our two-year-old in the supermarket and to our own ride on the plastic-card roller coaster grows more possible. Economic justice and living simply are a matter of proportion.

Concern for poor people becomes a way of life. Christopher did not newly discover our family's responsibility for others. A large family, we celebrate a great deal together—and at Christmas by *not* exchanging gifts among the adults. There is one gift for each of the grandchildren at our family gathering of forty or so. They receive other remembrances in their own homes prior to our coming together. The funds that would have formed a stack of bright boxes taller than the Christmas tree bring hope and comfort to those who need to know the love and gift of Jesus.

The Christmas celebration ripples across the months. Easter, the beginning of school, and Thanksgiving are some of the occasions of sharing with those who have less than we do. Some of the families have "adopted" a child or two whom they help through life's struggles. Every door is open to the stranger. As a family, we have been blessed and know the truth in the proverb, "Whoever is kind to the poor / lends to the LORD, / and will be repaid in full" (Proverbs 19:17). Sharing opens new horizons of political consciousness for changing the system, and many of the adults are involved.

Throughout the Scriptures, God's love and concern for poor people is a powerful current, illuminating our direction. No dark glasses of our choosing can dim that light. If we do not see, we are blind and lost, and we do not know who we are.

Fasting as Food

Fasting can be an emptying of self-desires
to be free to do God's will for us.

"Remember six months ago, when you visited us? You gently suggested that I try to get in touch with myself," Alice reminded me. "I wasn't quite sure what you meant, but we have known each other so long that I knew you saw beyond the person that others were applauding—the dutiful wife caring for her ill husband."

Alice and I had been young brides together, and we shared in the mysteries of child-rearing and later in the balancing on the tightrope between family and careers. What I had seen on that day, some months previous, was a person out of control. She was like an engine managing to keep on the track of what had to be done. But she was not only running out of fuel, she was acting more like a programmed robot than a woman who usually took charge of matters.

Alice had met the diagnosis of big, affable Bill's Alzheimer's disease with courage and love. As a nurse, she understood the implications but decided she would care for her husband as long as she could.

Her children and friends were quick to help, but she relentlessly maintained that Bill needed *her*. Within a year she had walked into a desert of the soul where relationships, even with God, were strained or nonexistent. Her alienation from life increased with alcohol, tranquilizers, and overeating.

My comment troubled her, and she spoke to her pastor. He suggested a retreat. At the retreat house, she chose to grapple with her situation in solitude and silence. "I had hidden my anger and fear for so long that I was in danger of losing my capacity to love and for life. As I began to examine the Alice of now, I wept over who I once was. Where had my laughter gone? What happened to the disciplined, aware person who frequently fasted for world peace? Most of all, where was the friend of Jesus who had a continuing daily conversation with him?

"I came face-to-face with the fact that I really didn't know who I was anymore. I was scared. I missed dinner the first day at the retreat house, and the next day's lunch. I couldn't get myself together enough to go out of my room. Without intending it, I was emptying my body as well my soul. I began to feel better and freer. Peace came back to me quietly and slowly.

"I returned home to change the rhythm of my life. I let go of many crutches. Now others help me with Bill, for I see that both he and they have that right. Prayer and God's peace nourish me, so alcohol and pills are not part of my routine. With the doctor's approval I fast frequently, a meal at a time.

"My days have become 'thank-yous' to the Lord for the beauty of life he has given us and the beauty that still exists, even in the pain. As the disease worsens, our caring becomes holy, and we share each other's grief. The most wonderful part is that the atmosphere is not morbid. It is surprising how much we laugh and hug each other!"

Alice's story illustrates that fasting can be an emptying of self-desires, to be free to do God's will for us. We usually link fasting with food. Some people fast from certain foods for cultural or religious reasons. The Scriptures speak of fasting from food by the early prophets, and we have the example of Jesus fasting as he prepared to do the will of his Abba. In our times, publicity is given to those heroic persons who undertake long fasts for the cause of justice. They are significant signs of the nobility of humankind as they sacrifice themselves, even to death.

Most of us are more like Alice, unthinkingly imprisoned by our appetites. But what should we give up? No one can tell us. Our life is unique, and it changes as we move through the years. Deep inside ourselves we know that continued gratification, however innocent in itself, will never really satisfy us. Even as our desires cry out for more, we are sickened in body and spirit. This is our cue to look to the prophets, to Jesus, and to Alice, and then to go apart to some quiet place so that we may cleanse ourself of that which is driving us and get in touch with who we are and what we have been called to. When we are in harmony, our appetites lose their power over us, and we can truly live life to the fullest. In this context, fasting makes good sense in our modern world.

The Mysterious Movements of Faith

Faith is a gift from God and, as a gift, we can refuse it.

Each time Joe and his daughter Helen were together, unsettling eruptions punctuated the atmosphere. Joe did not approve of the woman Helen had become. Her life as a successful fashion coordinator did not include a lot of things Joe thought it should. She refused to discuss the companions who occupied her glittering social life or why she did not attend church.

Out of the wisdom of a mother's heart, Pat tried to reason with her husband. "Helen has moved too fast to think, and the momentum is still absorbing her. Give her more time—she's only thirty. She has more growing to do."

Helen's nieces and nephews saw her as a shining star, questionable role model or not. She stayed within the family circle until her job escalated, and then she moved to New York. The calls home became less frequent, and she became the aunt who was more myth than reality.

Recently I saw her at the christening of her youngest sister's baby. This time she attended the church service, and I noticed that she repeated her baptismal vows along with the rest of us. Pat relaxed her usual anxious silence to tell me that the young parents had chosen Helen as the godmother only to learn that she was not eligible because she was not a practicing Catholic. Helen was furious, protesting that she had always been a Catholic. She even called the pastor, who explained the wisdom of such a ruling.

Helen remained with her parents for a few days after the christening. She visited Father Jim, who had been in her class in grade school. Because she had to cross the city to see him, it was not a casual meeting. We do not know the questions she asked or the answers she received, but we have hope that somewhere in her closely guarded heart the flame of faith still flickers. In James Fowler's study on faith development, Helen would likely be in stage four: beginning to question her overemphasis on success to the neglect of her commitment to God.

Faith is a gift from God and, as a gift, we can refuse it. Once accepted, however, it is up to us to pursue its mystery and to nourish its growth by our openness to and confidence in God. Depending upon our constancy, faith can be steel reinforcing our wholeness or a plume of smoke softly signaling what might be. Faith is a covenant with God that engages head, heart, and will. Growing in faith demands more than learning *about* God. Faith calls for a loving relationship, expressing itself in actions taught to us by the life of Jesus.

Just as we grow physically and emotionally, we also grow in faith. Growth takes place in stages, and within each stage there is an ebb and flow—snags, crises, spurts, and periods of calm.

At her yard sale, Emily saved her trusty trowel for poking in some future hanging basket, but the garage full of garden equipment gradually disappeared during the day. This was Bill and Emily's emancipation from the big yard surrounding the great old house. It was to be "turn the key and away we go, living from now on!" Forty some years of caring for children, pets, lawn, and roses were over. Dues had been paid, freedom won. They embraced their new life like toddlers splashing on a seashore.

They were called home from a golf outing when their twelve-year-old grandson, Greg, was hit on his bike. His life clung to the machines pumping at his bedside. Bill and Emily shared the vigil at the hospital. Finally, when Greg was out of danger, Bill shook his head. "We were sustained by so many kind and caring volunteers, mostly our age, sharing words of comfort as they went about their assignments. One day I spotted my former boss in a volunteer uniform. 'Why aren't you wading in some trout stream?' I asked. He laughed. 'Once in a while I still get the urge, but now that I can test my skill any day I want, it's no longer the thrill it used to be. Besides, my wife and I looked at our life and saw that we were busy about nothing. We're here two days a week, and we're happier now that we've taken the focus off ourselves and are helping other people.'"

Greg's accident proved a turning point for Bill and Emily. She candidly admitted: "We had three years of pampering ourselves, and maybe we had to go through that period to be free to really choose what we would do with the rest of our lives. It's back in the kitchen for us—the parish kitchen—where we are part of a group that cooks and delivers food for the homebound. I frankly don't know how these dear folks would make it without our group. It's a healthy condition for us to feel needed." On Fowler's scale of faith development, these retirees would to be at the stage where they are willing to pay the cost of being a contributing part of a community.

In its countless, coy disguises, pride is a stumbling block to growth in faith for most of us. Humility helps us let go and grow!

In his book *The God Who Fell from Heaven,* Father John Shea says it clearly and lyrically: "Our faith may be encapsulated in single stark statements like 'God is love,' but its implications burst slowly, like delayed fireworks, over the long days and fast years of our life."

The Awesome Mystery of Worship

They had stepped inside the mystery of the celebration,
and their smiles invited all of us to join them. Indeed,
a chain of smiles passed among the people.

A few years ago in a small, country parish, a couple sat in the pew in front of my husband and me: a tall man with a red neck as creviced as a creek bed parched by the August sun; her polyester jacket hitched up in the back to hug the hump of her spine. You could guess that their life had been hard, but they possessed a majesty that cannot be bought. They leaned to each other with tender familiarity, and, as the offertory time approached, he put his arm around her and said, "Now."

With trembling hands, they self-consciously and deliberately carried the gifts to the altar. The priest spoke a few words to them. They genuflected as much as their tired legs allowed and turned. Their faces shone on us. This seemingly simple couple who symbolically had offered the gifts of each of us had been able to surrender themselves totally. They had stepped inside the mystery of the celebration, and their smiles invited all of us to join them. Indeed, a chain of smiles passed among the people. Friends and strangers, as if discovering a secret together, were united.

There was something so rare and pure about the experience that I wondered what I could do to recapture again that sense of celebration, participation, and community. None of us can match the astonishing love of God for us, but could we not make the time of worship more reciprocal?

I began to ask different people, "What is there about the Mass that helps you worship better?" A widower replied: "The

friendliness of the congregation, especially at the sign of peace. I feel like I'm part of God's people and not so alone." Rita in Florida was enthusiastic about the music: "All those voices raised in praise together is awe-inspiring, and I find myself singing snatches of the hymns all week long." Many answered that it was the homily, "Especially if it personally hits home for me." For some others it was the Eucharist itself. "I wouldn't feel complete if I did not receive." A college student repeats the Prayers of the Faithful to his friends. "They connect our faith with the problems of the world and civic responsibility."

I have found that if I reflect on the readings of the Liturgy of the Word ahead of time, I have a better chance of bringing forth the truths that lay hidden in them. Then when I hear them proclaimed from the altar, they are not migrant thoughts passing by.

Almost everyone I questioned, when pressed a little further, agreed that the more people brought to the experience and the more open they were to participating, the more they received. Every so often, we are privileged through exceptional grace to know the fullness of celebration, participation, and community.

For example: It was noon; the funeral liturgy had begun at 10 a.m., but as the crowd of persons moved to the ice-glazed parking lot, no one complained about the time. Rather, they spoke of the unhurried beauty of the ritual celebrating the long life of a Christian whose active days began with the Eucharist and of the emotional richness of remembering what Frank had meant to each of us. Through stories taking us backward and forward in laughter and tears, Frank's son, Father Bob, had created a flawless link between his father's life and the age-old sacrifice of the passion and death of Christ. We had lost our sense of time as we entered into God's time.

We had come together because death had called someone we cherished. We were impelled beyond that purpose to clearly see that which we often gloss over. The liturgy calls each of us to our own death to self, so that a new person will go forth in peace to love and serve the Lord.

Later, at the cemetery, a man quietly mused, "That Mass really got to me. Frank lived what he believed. Most of us go through the motions, waffling between what God calls us to and our own selfishness. We live a kind of spiritual schizophrenia. In the long run, Frank's way is the only one that makes sense."

That man's brooding struggles with himself reminded me of an insight heard at a day of prayer. "At Mass we are not watching a 'Passion play.' We *are* the drama, and we become the Word of God when we live the truths proclaimed in the scriptural readings."

Caring Parish Families

The reality is that some families are not capable of loving support,
but parishes have begun to reinvent themselves
to be caring families.

Jane Howard wrote a warm and perceptive book, *Families,* the central premise of which is that families are so important to us that if we don't have one, we invent one. The reality is that some families are not capable of loving support, but parishes have begun to reinvent themselves to be caring families. Parishes are sending forth trained persons who are willing to walk with others on their troubled journeys in the same way that Christ did, with love, understanding, and assistance.

The stories that follow are but two examples of the mature sharing of the energies and resources of familial parishes motivated by extraordinary love.

The gaunt man lay in the hospital bed, his Adam's apple moving up and down angrily in his stringy neck. His fingers plucked spasmodically at the soft fuzz of the blanket. Only the eyes of this Alzheimer's patient were still, staring blankly. Gwen sat near the bed reading aloud. The sound of her pleasant voice seemed to soothe Sam.

Gwen is a member of Respite, a program in her parish. For three hours every Thursday afternoon, she stays with Sam in this cheery room that had once been the family's sunroom. Over many weeks, Gwen has been staying with Sam while Dorothy, his wife, enjoys a brief time for herself.

Another parishioner, who knew of the devastating situation at Sam and Dorothy's, had appealed to Thomasine, the person in charge of the Respite program in the parish. Thomasine contacted Dorothy and found a nearly exhausted woman valiantly trying to care for her beloved husband. Thomasine understood why Dorothy had not asked for help herself. She was emotionally caught in the inertia common to persons drained by fatigue in what seems to be a situation with no solutions.

Respite does not provide medical assistance. It offers hope, a rest, and some freedom for those who care for the patient. Respite also reinforces positive attitudes in the patients themselves. The parish advertises Respite weekly in the parish paper, but Thomasine knows that many who need their help are like Dorothy and unable to respond. "We depend on referrals of concerned parishioners or those in the community. All of our fifteen volunteers are busy, and we plan to recruit more in the fall. People are so generous, and our volunteers are of all ages. It's really the Lord's work we're doing."

The Stephen Ministry is another way that parishes become caring families. Stephen ministers are dedicated to "being there" for those who need the emotional support of one who understands and is willing to listen.

Gert lived in the same house over half of her eighty-nine years. Now, because arthritis has impaired her mobility, she resides in a nursing home. Even though she agreed to the move, she strains against the reality of her need and has become a cantankerous patient.

One of her former neighbors contacted Kathy, the coordinator of the parish's Stephen Ministry. "Gert could be happy there, but she needs someone to talk to who would understand her loneliness and fear. My bad heart prevents me from going very often, but I understand you have volunteers who could visit her. I wouldn't want the other neighbors to know. Gert has always been so proud and strong."

Kathy assured her that confidentiality is strictly observed by Stephen ministers. Kathy checked with the nursing home. They welcomed the potential help because their staff could not reach Gert. Kathy assigned a sensitive woman, Meg, who had helped others suffering the losses that come with relocation.

Meg reported to Kathy. "While standing in Gert's doorway, I felt like an unwanted guest. We eyed each other like novice aerialists on the highwire, unsure of what we were supposed to do next. My Stephen training gave me courage, and I was grateful that I had checked with Gert's neighbor friend for information. I said, 'I bring you news of the old neighborhood.' Silence. Gert's blue eyes were frigid. I moved into the pleasant room and offered a tiny bouquet of daisies. 'They're from my garden. You grew them too, didn't you?' The atmosphere softened. Gert said, 'There's a vase on the windowsill; get the water in the bathroom.'

"Gert spoke first about waking up at night afraid of the strange shadows, so many people, and strange foods. Once that was said, she began to remember persons and happy places, especially her honeymoon at Niagara Falls and her own yard that once bloomed with hollyhocks, nasturtiums, peonies, as well as the daisies. 'All gone now,' Gert cried. 'But they're alive in your memory,' I said. Gert said softly, 'I guess we carry who we are with us, and bring back the good things when we talk about them.'"

Meg and Gert continued to meet on a regular basis. Gert settled into the home, content that someone cared and knew of the good things that could not be taken from her.

Meg is in her second year of her three-year commitment to the Stephen Ministry. Before she began her assignments she completed fifty hours of training and is now preparing to attend a two-week session to become a leader herself. She will aid the parish's four other trainers in twice-a-month meetings with the ministers for support and counsel, praying together at the semiannual retreats, and training new ministers.

Parish programs such as Respite and Stephen Ministry know that healing happens when lives come together, motivated by love to answer a need. Their ministries are one-to-one, care-giver and care-receiver: a seamless interweaving of giving and receiving, receiving and giving.

The generous, dedicated people in all familial parishes must have prayed the words of Psalm 26:2: "Prove me, O LORD, and try me." God hears them and sends them forth to care for their brothers and sisters in Christ.

A Good Deed Is Never Exhausted

We do not know ourselves or others
until we invite the strangers to join us.

Widowed for fourteen years, Helen had sold linens at Sears and was now retired. She had a modest, predictable, tidy life. Nearly eighteen months ago, she took her elderly aunt into her home. The aunt had been hospitalized for depression and could not take care of herself. They had no other relatives. "My Aunt Mary had only Social Security. I could not stretch my income to cover a nursing home, and the alternative seemed wrong."

Helen continued. "At first I was amused and called her 'my little shadow,' for she was always at my side, smiling vaguely, twisting her fingers, smoothing her dress, and almost always silent. Then I began to be overcome with an emotional claustrophobia and felt so closed in at times that I was terrified. I realized I had relinquished something necessary for my own balance—my privacy and my freedom.

"I did go out, but always with Mary, as both she and I feared to leave her alone. It was not frequent, as she was uncomfortable in crowds. My attempts to interest her in television or sewing alone were resisted. She began to show a testy irritability that made the 'shadow' even more abrasive to my raw nerves.

"Last year during Lent, Mary suddenly said she had to make her Easter Duty. I think it was the good Lord intervening, for what happened brought new life to my life. While I was alone with Father in my own confession, I spoke of my anger at my captive situation. He listened sympathetically and said he thought the parish could help me in doing God's work.

"I had a call from a pleasant woman in the parish's Christian Service Commission. She listened to my story and came to the house with Brenda, Evelyn, and Ed. After several visits, the three gained Mary's confidence. Brenda, a former beautician, spends a half day a week with Mary, doing her hair, nails, and sometimes a facial. Evelyn and Ed, contemporaries in age to Mary, but buoyed by abundant optimism, come to 'gamble' each Friday evening. They have even lifted laughter out of Mary when she wins at Hearts.

"Mary will not likely ever recover, and I am still confined, but the bonds do not cut. I am able to be tender, for I'm seeing the wounded Jesus instead of a shell of a woman. Brenda, Evelyn, and Ed have taught me that a good deed is never exhausted; it whispers its life into others."

Sally and Carl had been attending marriage preparation classes for a short time at Sally's parish. Chuck and Kit Murray were working with them along with Father Ed. In their late twenties, Sally and Carl were successful, bright, on their way up, and a bit cool in their responses during the marriage sessions. Father Ed felt an underlying current between Carl and Sally, unrevealed perhaps even to each other. The three leaders continued without pressing uncomfortably, but waiting.

The moment came when Kit said that "marriage is a leap of faith, letting God take over." Carl leaned forward and said, "I can't do it, I'm not ready!" Then he dragged his feelings out of the hollows of his heart. "I love Sally, but I'm not sure I love her enough to live with the competition of her success. I don't want to lose her, but I can't gamble and risk causing our marriage to fail. God's got other things to do than worry about my inadequacies." Carl's honest, frightened stripping of himself was in stark contradiction to the confident young man they had known.

After the tears, Sally thanked them, and said that they would be in touch. The wedding was postponed, but Sally and Carl continued their relationship and seeing the Murrays. Once Carl had voiced his fears, they did not hover like vultures over him. He was further encouraged by Sally's obvious love of him for himself and not for his present or potential success. The Murrays and Father Ed were healthy influences on the couple, and in a year— five years ago—Sally and Carl were married. Carl had begun to realize that our own shortsightedness can prevent us from meeting God in the persons he sends to us and in ourself.

Jim had become a eucharistic minister partly because Peg, his wife, was often confined at home with arthritis. He felt that it was his responsibility and privilege to bring communion to her. As he made his rounds, Jim felt he needed something more to share with people. He joined an evening Bible study group to find a new dimension in his ministry. Prayers and the reading of the Word were shared, and he became a friend of the families.

Now that he has retired, Jim is one of the busiest eucharistic ministers in the parish. Jim prayerfully prepares for each visit, and the homebound eagerly await his arrival. He joins the families in their celebrations and in their sorrows. Quite often he is a pallbearer for his special friends. Jim shakes his head and smiles at his good fortune. "I looked forward to retirement with reluctance. The future days yawned with meaningless tasks. Now I experience life with a capital *L*. I am way beyond what I thought were going to be my limits. By reading the Scriptures daily and caring for others, I have transcended the man I was. Even though Peg can't always join me, we read and pray together. She's my backup at home."

The parish can be a means of revealing the mysteries of life. Like the disciples on the road to Emmaus, we do not know ourself or others until we invite the strangers to join us. In so doing we see with new eyes the needs of those around us. As a parish community we have strength greater then the sum of the individuals. The good deeds are never exhausted.

Leadership Cares

"Successful leadership is how you treat people."

Her voice is soft, her bearing modest, almost shy, as she steps forward to accept the award. Honors and appointments have been numerous, but she is too wise to be victimized by pride. She knows from experience that even if you try with all your heart, your efforts sometimes fall short.

Regina Rambeau once told me: "Acclaim is like cream on strawberries, which is nice but not necessary. You get only grumbles when you burn the toast."

Regina grew up learning the elaborate code of a black person living in a white society. She was the first black child in an exclusive Catholic school for girls. She has spent a lifetime wrestling with questions of human dignity and equality and charting the steps of what she could do about them.

Always active in her parish's human relations and interracial councils and boards, her most sustained effort began in the 1960s as the Catholic representative to Women in Community Service (WICS) in Detroit. In a short time she became director, national recruiter, and, later, a member of the national board. WICS is funded by the Federal Department of Labor to recruit, screen, and train young women, ages sixteen to twenty-one, to move beyond their past, to live and work productively.

In Regina's Great Lakes area, the majority of women being trained are black, and thousands have been sent proudly forth from the Detroit office. The immensity of the fruit of her commitment is brought home to her when she meets graduates. "I occasionally bump into someone who stops me and says, 'Twenty years ago you turned my life around!'" Regina adds, "I know what Eleanor Roosevelt said is true. 'The influence you exert is through your own life and what you've become yourself.' I have tried to be what I believe, but it is wearying. Equality moves forward, and then it moves back. Yes, it is wearying."

Dennis and Margaret's small parish teeters on the edge of town. Unity had been forfeited there by a faction of people who refused the changes in the church as if they were a corruption that undermined the Catholicism of their childhood. When Father Tom came as the new pastor, he set out with patience and sensitivity to defuse the land mines in the parish.

Dennis and Margaret stepped forward to help him. They were listening to the call of their own conscience and working out of the context of healing. "Volunteers for every job were scarce," said Dennis, "so we had to be flexible and willing to sacrifice."

They both spoke of the conscious presence of Christ in their life and the vocation to do what God is calling them to do. This knowledge gave them the emotional dexterity to serve and serve again without being defeated. They have been the unseen, un-sung helpers as well as parish council members, eucharistic min-isters, lectors, and ushers.

At forty, Margaret pledged to become a positive force in the lives of those she met. This promise has taken on a special poten-cy, for she is teaching CCD to the twelve- to fourteen-year-old youths of the parish. She is passing on an attitude of life as well as the faith and values that have sustained her.

Dennis is a meat cutter by profession, and Margaret a third-grade teacher in a public school. When asked about their prepa-ration and philosophy of leadership, Dennis lighted up with an Irish grin. "Life itself and those you have admired teach you throughout your life. Successful leadership is how you treat peo-ple." Margaret added: "Leaders should bring more interaction among groups in the parish and make a real effort to include everyone. And gratitude is essential. People think a thank-you note is a bonus when it should be a must."

This year at the paschal meal, a sense of invisible but real oneness floated through the small social hall as each person rec-ognized the imperishable beauty and awe of being a member of the people of God. The rapt pleasure on Margaret's face said: "Here is warm community. It's been worth the effort."

Regina, Margaret, and Dennis have no arrogance or smugness and deny any unusual qualities of leadership. Yet caring about people sends deep roots into the heart. Caring has no termination point. It grows as the person grows. It is the essence of Christian leadership and makes the ordinary, extraordinary!

Prophets Come Great and Small

*If some prophets can be compared to campfires,
others are lighthouses, dependable beacons lighting our way.*

In the Scriptures the prophets loom as giants set apart. People heard the word of God through them, and this is still true. They shine in history, helping us gain perspective about God, nature, and our own journey. I also believe that God sends us quiet prophets who speak to just a few persons, and perhaps only to one.

Some prophets are like campfires that you come upon suddenly and sit before to warm your soul. I recently chanced upon one such prophet in a restaurant. I was waiting to be served a late lunch in an uncrowded section when I observed a man, perhaps thirty-five. He had clearly stumbled across miles of unfriendly floors and was trying desperately to find acceptance in this place. It was apparent that his mind had ceased to grow in pace with his hulking body, but he applied himself with all the concentration of a tennis superstar in the finals of a major tournament.

He was being trained to be a busboy. As he removed the dishes, wiping each empty table with the antiseptic cloth, he held his tongue in the corner of his mouth just as a child does while trying to control crayons to stay inside the lines of a coloring book. He moved from table to table while his supervisor, a gentle young man in his twenties, quietly reminded him of certain procedures, such as replacing the wire container of salt and pepper in the same position on each table. The trainee would bend his head toward the supervisor, listen, nod, wipe his forehead with the back of his hand, and proceed.

I was standing outside another person's life, watching an act of heroism and nobility. I was inspired by the miracle before me. After some kind words and reminders, the supervisor left. Soon the trainee came to the table next to mine. When he had everything in place, I smiled and said, "You do good work." He looked frightened at first, but then smiled radiantly. His words tumbled out at an uneven pace. "I know God will take care of me, but I should try to help myself too."

As I paid my bill, I complimented the manager for giving the trainee a chance. He answered simply, "I did it because it seemed right, but in the few days he has been here, I have re-evaluated my life. The restaurant business is not for me. I am going back to get the degree I started in education so I can work with mentally challenged people."

If some prophets can be compared to campfires, others are lighthouses, dependable beacons lighting our way. I came from a family of such prophets. They counseled me perceptively, giving me room for my natural independence and curiosity to break free. I was ready then, when I entered college, to listen to the wise woman who became my lifelong friend, mentor, and prophet, Sister Honora, IHM, president of Marygrove College.

Some students got a case of nervous hives when they saw their name posted for a visit with her, but I anticipated the visits with pleasure. Our meetings, for example, might be a progress report on my work at an African-American community center where I taught art to the children and helped the parents organize a neighborhood club. Sister Honora was global in her view of education and the need for community service. My effort was an experiment for the college, and she was monitoring it carefully.

About the middle of my sophomore year, Sister directed the conversation away from our usual reporting or sharing of thoughts about God, current affairs, and books that she had encouraged me to read. Her statement came out quick as an arrow without warning. "I understand the sisters are badgering you about entering the convent." I felt taut and strained. I did not want the sisters to be in trouble, but it was true that they had formed a circle around me with many strings pulling me to the convent door.

I simply looked at her. She had her answer. Her voice was firm. "Don't worry. I know they mean well. In fact, they are not wrong, but they are seeing only one side of the prism. I am sure you are called to bring Christ to the marketplace. You belong in the world, not the convent as we know it today in the 1940s."

She saw what my immaturity blurred. She set my gears in motion. No matter how clumsy I have been at times, I have tried not to be insulated from the world and the mission she showed me as mine. Sister has been gone for some years, but her lighthouse signal transcends time.

God is light, as Saint John declares in his Gospel. God gives some persons varying intensities of light. Some have the light of a galaxy, others a campfire, and some a lighthouse, but all lead us away from darkness. We need only open our eyes.

Seeking to Make a Difference

*"'We will be judged not by our good intentions
but by our actions to ease the suffering of the Christ
represented in each of our neighbors.'"*

Since Vatican Council II, church leaders have stressed that the fight for social justice is an essential element in our quest for individual sanctification and salvation. So I have often wondered how people felt about their personal responsibility for justice and what they were doing about it. At various meetings I began to ask.

Most everyone expressed some concern. They prayed for a better world, contributed funds to one charity or another, and worked in soup kitchens or nursing homes. Some admitted to being afraid of becoming involved with poor people; some thought they were too busy or felt "the job should be left to the professional agencies and the government."

I did hear many heroic stories of those who wanted to make a difference. The following is the story of Tony, a silver-haired, vigorous, retired businessman.

"Every night it was the same assault on our senses, with the TV news focusing on mangled corpses heaped helter-skelter on strange, war-torn streets; frightened children who had known the nightmare of abuse; homeless persons, seemingly as disposable as the rubbish in the trash cans they rummaged through; a bullet-riddled teenager shown dead in an emergency room as the commentator attributed the tragedy to another gang fight in the world of drugs.

"One evening I asked my wife, Helen: 'Has seeing so much inhumanity robbed us of our humanity? How can we keep sitting here watching injustices that cry to the heavens and not do more than give money. I don't know what to do, but . . .' And my voice trailed off.

"Helen pressed her hands against her forehead and shakily said, 'I've been thinking about it too and praying that God would penetrate my own numbness.'

"Helen's prayers were answered at Mass the following Sunday with a message that did reach us.

"Father Steven was struggling with the sadness in our parish over the senseless death that week of a dedicated woman parishioner. She was killed as she drove to a nearby mall in the early evening by a driver who had gambled with his ability to drive after a long, alcoholic happy hour.

"At the homily, Father Steven began: 'We cannot eliminate the formidable hurt of the Burns family, but we can channel our shock and anger into awareness and action as responsible instruments for the cause of justice. The destruction of a human life by a drunk driver is a terrible injustice, but it is only one of many that exist in an increasingly dysfunctional society.

"'Human rights and the dignity of the human person are constantly being violated, not just in remote parts of the world but in the poor and oppressed in our community, by the barriers we have erected between races and classes, by allowing profit to be the incentive for human progress, and by indifference to public policy formation. The Christ we say we love and follow is suffering all around us. Don't we see this? When we die we will be judged not by our good intentions but by our actions to ease the suffering of the Christ represented in each of our neighbors.

"'It is true our parish has responded to many needs, but just as in the Scriptures, the laborers are too few. The parish council has planned a meeting on Tuesday evening with the hope that more of you will become active in a personal commitment to the cause of justice in our world.'

"Father Steven spoke more about helping the Burns family and suggested that we stand in solidarity against drunk driving by displaying the red ribbons advocated by Mothers Against Drunk Driving (MADD). He concluded with, 'I used to think the sin of sins was pride, but I have come to realize that as evil as pride can be, apathy can be worse.'

"Helen and I attended that large meeting two years ago. Since then we have become more and more involved in programs we didn't know existed. I stopped being a management consultant for a fee and now volunteer my services to struggling little businesses to help them get on their feet. Helen has revived her teaching skills, working one-on-one with school dropouts whose inadequacies would have kept them forever among the hopeless poor. Whatever we do, we get back more than we give. My favorite job is being a foster grandfather for a class of first graders in a poor, black neighborhood. I do just what grandfathers are supposed to do—listen and love. My little folks are starved for both. Two mornings a week I help the teacher by giving individual attention to slower-learning children, and during noon lunch time we read books and talk about the stories. I learn much from our conversations, and I encourage the children to be the beautiful persons God has called them to be.

"In March we decided not to go to Florida. Instead, we joined a group of younger couples in the parish in the renovation of a small apartment building that the city was going to condemn. I figured if President Carter could work with his hands restoring and building housing for the poor, so could I. We worked through Habitat for Humanity International, with whom our parish has agreed to become a covenant church. Six families now live in what would have been destroyed. They take great pride in their homes, for each family labored right along with us. They have a sweat equity in what is now theirs.

"We still display our red ribbons as a sign of the deep commitment that penetrates the very lives of our people in their awareness and action. Many of our college students have shifted their career directions to political science, legislative lobbying, social work, community development, and others that will make a difference."

Tony and his parish are powerful examples of loving God in each person and therefore fulfilling the great commandments. Is it necessary to be personally touched by injustice before becoming committed to justice? Actually, no one is immune to injustice. As Saint Paul tells us, "If one member suffers, all suffer together with it; if one member is honored, all rejoice together with it" (1 Corinthians 12:26). This is what our humanity is about. This is what our Christianity is about.

Transforming Intimacy

Instant intimacy is not one of the wedding gifts.

Intimacy is more than sharing a bed or a candlelit table. The intimacy of which we will speak is based on love, commitment, reverence, and maturity. One of the joys that intimacy should provide is the elevation of our sense of being special. It has the power to transform the ordinary elements of life into something exciting. It forces us to see the mystery and beauty in common events such as a shared, simple meal, a walk together, an unexpected call, a touch in passing, a glance exchanged in a crowd. These moments become ripe with emotion and different from others because a knowing love and trust create the wonder and shelter the promise of continuity.

The concept of continuance is necessary for intimacy. When the bride and groom walk down the aisle after promising themselves to each other in the sacrament of matrimony, instant intimacy is not one of the wedding gifts awaiting them. Achieving intimacy is a gradual movement of two separate "I's" into a "We." No matter what the age of the couple, intimacy takes time. The movement is more graceful if the persons already know themselves and are willing to take the time to discover the other while revealing their innermost self. It is a fortunate couple who, especially in the early stages, recognize God's healing presence in their life as they struggle to achieve their maturity.

Sexual intimacy is a vital part of a couple's life, but it is not the only means to intimacy or even the most important, despite our modern preoccupation with sex and with making sexual love-making an end in itself.

Sara, an acquaintance of one of my children, came to visit me. She was troubled, but articulate in her analogy. "There is a dogwood tree in my yard that should be in full bloom, but a blue spruce has prevented its natural full growth. In nature, the strong survive. I guess that's the way it is in marriage too. Harry, my husband, takes what he wants and gives what he wants to give. We were physically attracted to each other—in fact, we still are—but lovemaking only satisfies my body. It's not enough, after five years of marriage. He doesn't know me, and I can't say I know him. Each time I try to talk about 'us,' he changes the subject. I feel so alone. I feel used."

I suggested that she and Harry see a therapist. After Sara threatened to leave him, Harry agreed to go with her. Now Sara and Harry are progressing to a stage of slow and painful self-disclosure. They are not only discovering who the other is, they are finding themselves. Since they both had a poor self-image, they are reveling in the wonder of themselves and each other!

Connie and I met at a bridal shower. The impish grin on her plain face made her age a question. She could be forty-five, but I suspected she had known many more years of living. She was retiring from a job she enjoyed, as was her husband. I impulsively asked why.

She replied with the candor sometimes prompted by casual meetings. "My husband and I want to know each other better, to discover and rediscover the world, and to do things together. We have the dream of working with illiterate people and helping them enter the wonder of ideas and wisdom awaiting them in reading books."

I pressed on. "Have you been married long?" Her reply put aside my thought of a brief relationship. "Over thirty years. We reached a turning point after our five children were on their own. We realized we are happiest, most fulfilled, when we're together, so we decided to take charge of our life and not just drift along to the expected retirement. What has made our marriage such fun is that while we are both independent, different persons who need their own space, we feel free to be ourselves with each other. Our love flows into every nook and cranny of our lives. Our advice to the couples we counsel in the pre-Cana program is to establish a trust relationship and then listen to the nuances floating around the needs expressed, whether it is to change jobs or make love in the afternoon. Whatever our responses to each other, they should always—as much as they can—say 'I love you.'"

A Matter of Priorities

She too was busy with many things, but the core from which all that tremendous energy radiated was her focus on God.

Mary of Bethany, sister of Martha and Lazarus, was not one of my favorite Scripture characters. I saw her as a pastel personality, insulated from the reality swirling around her. Now Martha—she with the bearing of a lioness—I saw as a woman of reds and purples, very responsive to life. There she was in her kitchen mixing the lentils and onions with olive oil, waiting on the table at the home of Simon, and setting out to find Jesus when Lazarus lay dead and Mary sat at home weeping.

I am sure that both Mary and Martha loved Jesus as the Messiah and as a friend. He certainly loved them and warmed to their hospitality. Why then, in Luke 10:41–42, when Martha came bustling with irritation from the kitchen to have Mary help her and leave the circle of those sitting at the feet of Jesus, did he say to Martha, "Martha, Martha, you are worried and distracted by many things; there is need of only one thing. Mary has chosen the better part, which will not be taken from her"? I kept asking myself, were they not both serving him in their own way?

The great parable stories were born from reality but reached for something beyond. That truth-beyond is hard to grasp, for mystery often defies logic.

As a young mother, the story's lesson had no resonance with my own life of new babies, endless meals to cook, and small wedges of volunteer service. I was anxious and upset with many things for which I had no options. The feisty Martha in me felt the Gospel was a put-down of women. Mary was a cop-out.

However, as I pursued the Scriptures further, logic did burn through some of my fog. Mary *had* to be very unusual. Jesus had called her, a woman, to be a disciple. In being so named, she was privileged to sit among the men at the feet of the teacher. Jesus consistently broke taboos about women's roles and was trying to tell Martha of the better way open to her as well.

I also discarded my pale image of Mary when I connected her in John's Gospel (12:1–4) with the woman at the banquet who brought the expensive perfume to pour over Jesus' feet in an extravagant and courageous testimony to his greatness. We do not know her reaction to the astonishment and anger of the other disciples for squandering money better spent on the poor. She must have felt it well worth her sacrifice and effort when Jesus said, "Truly I tell you, wherever the good news is proclaimed in the whole world, what she has done will be told in remembrance of her" (Mark 14:9).

My Aunt Ruth revealed a greater portion of the mystery of the parable to me. She knew who she was as she received the Eucharist each morning and spent the rest of the day prayerfully serving God's people. She was a spiritual juggler sustained by divine grace. She too was busy with many things, but the core from which all that tremendous energy radiated was her focus on God.

I suppose to some she seemed a typical Martha. She was a legendary teacher of English and public speaking in the Detroit schools, but she pulled her students up into an ascent of understanding of themselves and a value system that respected all human persons. When she died in her eighties, the distant world of her classrooms was represented at her funeral by students she had touched thirty or more years earlier.

Aunt Ruth taught catechism for fifty years, conscripting me into the process while I was still in high school. She knew how to delegate, for she was a leader who founded a Catholic library, the Sodality Union in Detroit, and so many other organizations and projects that they would fill pages.

A physically beautiful woman, she chose to remain single. Her Mary side gave the extravagant gift of herself to uniquely serve her God. Even when exhaustion crept in with age, she found new ways to serve. After daily Eucharist, she began her pilgrimages to the hospitals, nursing homes, and an occasional funeral. She visited friend and stranger alike: stroking hands, consoling the be-reaved, listening, encouraging, and praying to whomever was their God. She was an accepted, welcome, unofficial chaplain who brought the Good News. And she too will not be forgotten in our time.

Unlike mystery stories, the mystery of God is never totally re-vealed. Through the years, I think that I have isolated the lesson Jesus was giving to Martha when he spoke about her worrying and fretting "about so many things" and about Mary's better way. It's a matter of priority: Jesus. Jesus was the priority my Aunt Ruth lived by all along.

Reconciliation

How many of us can say we have not been the prodigal son or daughter to some degree or another?

The old man laid the small bunch of flowers, still wrapped in their supermarket tissue, gently on the grave. He stood there for a short time and then walked away. Since the old man had asked earlier for directions, the cemetery attendant took notice of him. He was visiting the grave of a young woman who had died some years before.

As he was leaving, the old man stopped to thank the attendant. He turned to go and then, seemingly prompted by the dredging up of something buried deep inside him, said quickly: "She was my daughter. I demanded a lot from her, and she ran away. I was too proud to go after her, and as time passed, the hurt seared my heart. For a long time, I didn't feel much of anything. My days are fewer now, and I knew I could not go before I told her I loved her and asked her forgiveness. I did not expect she would be gone. I hope she can hear me, even if it is too late and so little. At least I made some peace with myself."

We can contrast this with the Scripture story of the prodigal son who returns, repenting his wasted life. The father, hearing of his son's journeying home, has a lavish banquet prepared and personally runs out to embrace his son (Luke 15:11–32). In telling this story, Jesus was speaking about all lost persons who are groping their way back and of the welcoming compassion of God for them. We can identify with this story of hope because how many of us can say we have not been the prodigal son or daughter to some degree or another?

The old man spoke of making peace. Peace. We talk about it in global terms. Yet, first it must be personal. We need to talk about both peace and justice *with* reconciliation, for neither is achieved when a person or a people are at odds with another. How many people are suffering from the pain of needing forgiveness or from being imprisoned by stubbornly refusing to forgive? How many causes for peace and justice shred lives because people do not attempt to listen or negotiate? Consequently, the oppressed become the oppressors.

In some instances, we separate our reconciliation with others from our relationship with God. Jesus made clear that no matter how we rationalize, this is not acceptable. We cannot embrace

God with one arm and cradle our personal angers, hostilities, and pettiness in the other. "So when you are offering your gift at the altar, if you remember that your brother or sister has something against you, leave your gift there before the altar and go; first be reconciled to your brother or sister, and then come and offer your gift" (Matthew 5:23–24).

We may intend or wish to be reconciled but not have the guts within us to do so. Reconciliation is not an attitude or an action that goes with the flow of today's life. It calls us to stop and even go back. It demands change. Each reaching out in hesitant forgiveness to give or receive, each patching up of torn relationships, and each uneasy embrace is hard won. Reconciliation may be the way to peace of mind and restored love, but it cuts against the grain of how we are: our vulnerability to being hurt and our proud resistance in admitting that we are wrong. Forgetting coupled with forgiving, changing coupled with intending, are hard dynamics to integrate.

When people are in continuous presence, such as a husband and a wife, a parent and a child, coworkers, or groups living together, forgetting can seem an insurmountable challenge. Reminders of what we are trying to forget can spread like corrosive acid from batteries left too long. The power is gone, but the acid still burns. We can allow ourselves to be turned inward, miserably living in the past, or we can bring about a true acceptance of what happened and allow the Christ of Calvary to empty and reshape us with the courage of Paul. "I have been crucified with Christ; and it is no longer I who live, but it is Christ who lives in me. And the life I now live in the flesh I live by faith in the Son of God, who loved me and gave himself for me" (Galatians 2:19–20).

Even moved by God's power, we will live in the same world, with the same problems, but as we strive to constantly become closer to God our change will come. With this transformation, the joy of living flows again, as such that "no one will take [it] from" us (John 16:22). Then we will know what reconciliation is about. We will be different persons: free of ourselves, respecting all others and tuning to their needs. Unlike the old man in the cemetary, we will not walk in loneliness. Our companions will be all those who have discovered that reconciliation leads us from the cross to the full glory of Easter.

Every Story a Wonder Story

As she spoke, she was what her past taught her to be—
a window to God.

Daisy was rightly named. She required little attention from her sickly mother or her overworked father. She roamed the fields around her small, midwestern town and found her identity among the grasses and small creatures. She heard about God at Saint John's School, but the Creator was already her companion in the humming silence of nature.

Daisy worked as a cashier in the supermarket after high school, but longed for more knowledge. In an evening literature course at the community college, she met Michael, her teacher, who was impressed with her journal entries that beat with the pulse of the land. He became attracted by Daisy's simplicity and goodness. As they saw each other oftener, their age and educational differences melted under the warmth of their feelings.

They had been married five years when Michael was elected to their parish council's education commission. Part of the council's orientation was a day of recollection for members and their spouses. Daisy went but was not prepared for the faith-sharing part of the day. She felt inadequate to speak before people whom she imagined to be better educated and more capable of expressing themselves. Yet she did not want to embarrass Michael by remaining silent.

She was the last of the group to speak. Haltingly, she began to talk of God's presence in all created things and in her life. The group shared laughter as she spoke of the comic antics of the horny toad, her admiration of the genius of the beavers at the dam, and her sense of confidence in God's protection as lightening splintered the oak tree on the hill. As she spoke, she was what her past taught her to be—a window to God. Her peacefulness rested on the inspired group. They had seen a vision of creation their eyes had not known.

Each time we tell or hear a story of faith with reverence and honesty, we frame our life, find meaning and value in the jumble of events happening to us, and remind ourself of our progress in finding Jesus and following him.

Telling our stories is part of our tradition as a people. The stories of the Scriptures were told by believers around campfires on cold desert nights, in upper rooms, and on fishing boats. Our own stories are directly connected to those stories.

When faith stories are shared today, the group leader should urge everyone to make the storytelling a free-flowing conversation. The climate of prayerful reflection can help free participants of smug self-importance. Every story is a wonder story, each a glimpse of the vision of God among us. There will be stories of search, struggle, change, confrontation, denial, and unexpected peace. Each story must be treated with respect for the teller's courage and integrity.

I remember Eric. He approached the RCIA catechetical sessions like a starving man invited to a banquet. However, he was a discerning learner who probed and prodded the information until he could consume it. Guarded about himself, he revealed only the essentials until it came time for the group to share what prompted them to be there. He listened intently, noting the loving acceptance given each speaker. At his turn, he asked the group's understanding for what he called "a mystical experience."

"My life was a haphazard blur of work, play, and no serious commitments. One night last summer, I was driving home in a bad rainstorm. I skidded off the road into a ditch, hit something, and blacked out. I dazedly awoke to a woman rapping on my window. She could see I was bleeding and asked me to open the door. She pulled me out of the car, dragged me up to her car, tied something around my head. All I can remember is that she was young and dressed in white. Before I passed out again, I asked her who she was. She laughed and said, 'Just call me Miss Samaritan.'

"When I awoke in the hospital, she was gone. The emergency people had all my belongings, but they had not found out who she was other than that she was a nurse. Some assumed she was part of the staff. I investigated but found no trace of her. It bothered me. I began to think about what she had called herself. I read the Bible and even started to pray for the first time since I was a child. Like a window blind being opened, I saw God's goodness in the presence of the young woman. She saved my life, physically and spiritually. That's why I'm here. I really believe I was touched by the hand of God."

Then Eric added very softly, "Why me? I didn't care about him, but I'm thankful he cared about me."

The Young Old

Ages sixty-five and on can be a glorious autumn when the beauty of the moment is savored and the future is rich with promise.

Recently I rode an antique carousel and vanished from the world into a reverie with the child within me. Entranced, I moved up and down, round and round, riding every lion, horse, and frog whose reins I had ever held. I came back to the present only when the oompah-pah wound down and the mirrors of the central column stopped reflecting like a kaleidoscope. I enjoyed myself as much as I had at five or fifteen—in fact, more so, for at age sixty-nine I could embrace uncomplicated joy and give in to it.

Like most persons, when I was young I dreamed of what I would be when I grew up. In middle age, I pedaled so fast to keep up with family and career that I didn't always take the time to reflect on the beauty of what I had just experienced. Now in semiretirement, I have the gift of time—time for the unplanned, especially for the people who flow through my life: family, friends, and, often, unexpected strangers who need to tell their stories and of their groping for meaning and God to a gentle, unhurried ear.

I see this period not as stepping back from, but as stepping into, life. I am not alone. Just as pioneers sought better lives and pushed the frontiers of America farther and farther in all directions, most of today's mature persons have refused to accept a preordained number of years to describe old age. If blessed with fairly good health, the winter of life does not bring its chill until well into the eighties, if then. Ages sixty-five and on can be a glorious autumn when the beauty of the moment is savored and the future is rich with promise.

By this age, living has brought a certain wisdom. There is a letting go of the driving egoism that damages our perspective, and most persons have been able to shed the stains of old hurts and guilts and look upon the past with the beginning of understanding. This wisdom enables the mature adult to cope with life's reversals and helps to heal the spirit when tragedy strikes.

I grant you that not everyone is prepared to enter into this period with grace. We all know dreary, peevish persons whose sourness fouls their view of everything. They are in the minority, I have found. Let me tell you of a couple of persons whose spirit has cast a warm and tender light.

Paul, a retired doctor, was tired of reading hollow words about doing something about the growing illiteracy. He took a course on teaching basic literacy and now is teaching three persons on a one-to-one basis. He met them through the clinic where he is a volunteer. Paul's smile cut across his face like a beam of sunshine when he explained, "This is as thrilling as delivering a new baby, for I am bringing new life and hope to three persons who have had little chance for living fully in this world." Paul is eighty-two and keeps going!

My father battled cancer for thirty-five years. He was a formidable warrior, and he did not fall until he was seventy-six. A successful industrialist, after retirement he poured his energies into charitable endeavors and political action, especially welfare reform. Being in and out of his home almost daily, I could see a man still growing. His interior life expanded like a tree reaching for God. His life became a prayer, and he placed himself in the hands of his intimate friend, Jesus. When his time came, he was not afraid.

This age is continually carving new lifestyles. My Aunt Florence and a small group of longtime friends moved into a low-rise apartment complex for persons of all ages rather than live in an adult residence. Each has his or her individual apartment unit and individuality. However, they are conscious that their separate streams of life join the others to become the river of the caring community.

Without being intrusive, they know each other's whereabouts and state of health. Together they often attend church, shop, and visit the beauty parlor. Despite varying setbacks of illness and economics, they seem to be able to will themselves anew each day for their work at various agencies and organizations. Their life is full, and their rocking chairs seldom occupied. They are free to reverence each day as a gift.

Is This All There Is?

*"Success brought me many things,
but nothing to nourish the spirit."*

When I was young, my Grandmother Ouellette came each fall to help my mother can chili sauce. I remember the wonderful odors that filled the warm kitchen, but most impressive to me was the ritual of stirring and tasting for the just-right flavor. They had practiced their art so many times that they knew when the proper spices had met the variation-challenge of that year's tomato crop.

Living a good, full life is a little like making chili sauce. Until we have experienced a certain amount of conscious practice in living and getting to know ourselves, it is hard for most of us to know when we have reached a just-right formula. Muddling through life is more common than we like to admit.

Jean was a top real-estate broker for a large commercial firm. In her early thirties, she had delayed forming close relationships because of extensive travel and concentration on her career. Three years ago, in a distant city, she ignored a painful cough until her body could no longer support her will to continue. Pneumonia took over.

During her recuperation an old song, "Is That All There Is?" ran through her mind. Weakened and reflective, she stirred her memories and tasted the meaning of her present life. "It was a bitter time for me. I had to admit that my success was all I had. Success brought me many things, but nothing to nourish the spirit. In my frightened, sometimes disgusted, confusion, I began to talk to a nurse who was especially caring. I ranted my anger and resentment about my emptiness and the mess I was making of my life.

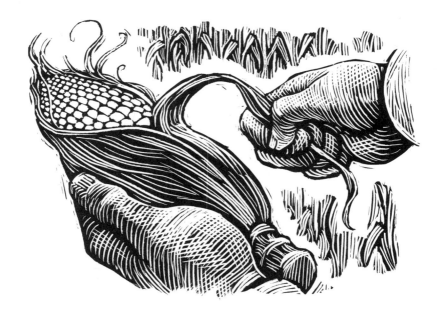

She listened, comforted me, and finally said, 'Let go, or you'll never be healed.' I knew it wasn't my body alone of which she spoke. Those times spent with her and in the quiet of my room helped me to see a fresh meaning to life and to gain an awareness of the holy. Even though we rarely referred to God, I felt God in her. The day I left the hospital my nurse friend gave me her address and phone number and asked me to keep in touch. I had begun the long road back to life."

Jean returned to her job, but it no longer consumes her. The structure and perspective of her life have opened to embrace more intimately her family and friends, to return to her potter's wheel, to teach minority groups the intricacies of real estate, and to walk with God in her everyday experiences. Jean's family, who had stood painfully by as they watched her soar, welcomed her back to family celebrations. At Christmas, they gloried in Jean's presence rather than her usual generous presents.

There are those who through some wondrous grace manage easily to hear God's call for them, like Steve. "I wouldn't want any other kind of life. Every spring when the bean crop starts sprouting, I feel I'm in partnership with God. In the summer, no woman's hair has more beauty than the silk on my corn. You might say that the land and I have a kind of love affair. Together we bring life and happiness to a lot of people. Sure, a farmer's life is hard, but it's real and important. I'm the third generation on this farm, and my kids and grandkids are part of it too. My sons and daughter studied at the university, and we win prizes at the state fair. We don't have a lot of money, but we can't complain."

A few years ago, around Christmas, Steve's doctors sent him to Florida after a heart bypass operation. Steve says, "That's when I really nearly died. I just didn't fit in. I missed the family and all the celebrations we always have—cutting down the big spruce and decorating it, singing carols, the little kids' giggling when they know I'm Santa. I know Joseph's feeling on Christmas Eve. I was a stranger in a strange land."

For many years I have gone out of my way to buy Steve's harvest and relish his friendship. Last year, when he learned that I was buying the large amounts for an inner-city parish soup kitchen, he loaded my car with his own contributions. He added some flowers to give away, "to feed the soul." He's a man at peace with himself and his life.

Sadly, some folks don't quite get around to achieving any harmony between their psychological and spiritual needs. The noise of the world drowns out their inner discord. Afraid of missing something, they career through life like a drunken bee, tasting everything. Often they end up as cantankerous oldsters, dripping poison as they continue their now desperate search for what they know not.

The fortunate ones generate an excitement about living. They are great to have around for simply being themselves. They have a sense of personal worth and personal responsibility. They know where they fit in their world and are concerned and curious about other people and conditions beyond themselves. They have their share of pain and sadness but, in knowing their weakness as well as their strength, they turn, without embarrassment, to God and persons for help. If you ask them what the good life is, they push aside things and dwell on values such as love, peace, beauty, truth, and goodness. The formulas vary, but whatever they are, they have become just right for them.

Index

Acknowledgments (continued)

The extract on pages 19 and 20 is from *Hamlet Prince of Denmark,* by William Shakespeare, in *The Complete Works,* edited by Alfred Harbage (Baltimore: Penguin Books, 1969), page 962. Copyright © 1969 by Penguin Books.

The first extract on page 30 is from *Selected Poetry of Jessica Powers,* edited by Regina Siegfried and Robert F. Morneau (Kansas City, MO: Sheed and Ward, 1989), page 55. Copyright © 1989 by Sheed and Ward.

The second extract on page 30 is from *Redemptor Hominis,* by John Paul II, in *The Papal Encyclicals, 1958–1981,* edited by Claudia Carlen (Wilmington, NC: McGrath Publishing Company, 1981), number 77. Copyright © 1981 by Claudia Carlen.

The extract on pages 32 and 33 is from *Meditations with Teresa of Ávila,* preface and versions by Camille Anne Campbell (Santa Fe, NM: Bear and Company, 1985). Copyright © 1985 by Bear and Company.

The extracts on pages 55 and 61 are from *Prayertimes with Mother Teresa, A New Adventure in Prayer Involving Scripture, Mother Teresa, and You,* by Eileen Egan and Kathleen Egan (New York: Image Books, 1989), pages 15 and 73, respectively. Copyright © 1989 by Eileen Egan and Kathleen Egan.

The extract on page 62 is from *On Human Work,* by John Paul II (Washington, DC: United States Catholic Conference, 1981), number 85. Copyright © 1981 by the United States Catholic Conference.

The first extract on page 85 is from *Pastoral Constitution on the Church in the Modern World* (Gaudium et Spes), by the Second Vatican Council (Washington, DC: National Catholic Welfare Conference, 1965), number 43. Copyright © 1965 by the National Catholic Welfare Conference.

The second extract on page 85 is from *The Divine Milieu,* by Pierre Teilhard de Chardin (New York: Harper Torchbooks, 1968), page 64. Copyright © 1960 by William Collins Sons and Company, Ltd., London, and Harper & Row, Publishers, Incorporated, New York.

The extract on page 97 is from *Economic Justice for All: Catholic Social Teaching and the U.S. Economy,* by the National Conference of Catholic Bishops (Washington, DC: United States Catholic Conference, 1986), number 23. Copyright © 1986 by the United States Catholic Conference.

The extract on page 105 is from *The God Who Fell from Heaven,* by John Shea (Niles, IL: Argus Communications, 1979), page 19. Copyright © 1979 by Argus Communications.